UNDERSTANDING
Ethics and Ethical
Decision-Making

UNDERSTANDING
Ethics and Ethical
Decision-Making

Case Studies and Discussions

VINCENT ICHEKU

BSc (Hons), PGCE, PGDipl. (Law), M.Phil., PhD

Senior Lecturer in Ethics and Law
Faculty of Health and Social Care
London South Bank University

Library of Congress Control Number: 2011914487
ISBN: Hardcover   978-1-4653-5130-2
                Softcover   978-1-4653-5129-6
                Ebook   978-1-4653-5131-9

This book was printed and marketed in United States of America by:

Xlibris Corporation
1663. Liberty Drive
Bloomington, IN 47403
Tel: +0800-644-6988,
Fax: 44-203-006-8880

To order additional copies of this book, contact:
Xlibris Corporation
www.xlibrispublishing.co.uk
Orders@xlibrispublishing.co.uk
302321

CONTENTS

Acknowledgements

I have many people to thank for making the publication of this book a reality. First, my wife, Chinell, a specialist nurse practitioner, for her suggestions on many aspects of ethical decision making framework in nursing practice; second, my children Sally-Anne, Genevieve, and William for their help with the typing of my notes.

I am indebted to all my nursing and social work students since 2008 who have given feedback on many aspects of this book, especially on the case study discussions. I am grateful to my colleagues, in particular Jane Murphy, a principal lecturer who encouraged me during one of our appraisal meetings to focus on research and publication for both my personal and professional development. The target agreed for the publication of this book was 2011 and meeting the target gave me a good sense of fulfilment. I am most grateful to Markella Boudioni, faculty senior research fellow, for reading my original draft, giving me advice, and encouraging me. I am also very grateful to many other colleagues, including Veda Johnson, for reading the entire script with valuable comments on the ethical practice in nursing; Charles Koranteng for leading the ethics and law unit successfully with me over many years; Jane Horrex and Sue Lattimer for reviewing many parts of my script and sharing their valuable experiences on ethical issues in nursing. My huge appreciation goes to Wijaya Mallikaaratchi for reviewing parts of the book's original script and giving his very useful feedback on ethical issues in social work practice. I would also like to thank Karen Sanders, senior lecturer, Adult Nursing and Midwifery, for constructive feedback on my paper, 'The SIAC Model of Ethical Analysis', presented to Ethics Special Interest Group, Health Sciences and Practice, Higher

Education Academy at University of Southampton. I am most grateful to Michelle Evans, senior lecturer, Learning Disability/Mental Health Nursing and Social Work, for the valuable feedback on Chapter 2 and social work case study discussion in Chapter 8.

I am also very grateful for the contribution made by colleagues from sister universities, particularly Jude Ibe, principal lecturer and programme leader, Department of Family Care and Mental Health, University of Greenwich, for reviewing some parts of my script, sharing his valuable experiences, and writing the foreword page to this book; Dr Patrick Okonta, research fellow, University of East London, for critically reviewing my original draft and for giving useful suggestions on structure.

I would like to thank Zarah Smith and Rhea Villacarlos of Xlibris Publishing Corporation for their support and utmost politeness with which they dealt with my numerous enquiries. I am most grateful to the entire Xlibris team for editing this book and for a job well done.

The overall strength of this book lies on the numerous literature on the subject of ethics, your encouragement and influence of those striving for excellence in the delivery of ethical knowledge to nursing and social work students. Once again, I am indebted to all of you and many others whose scholarly work inspired the writing of this book.

Finally, I commend the book to you all whilst accepting that all errors and limitations are entirely my fault.

Foreword

It was a great pleasure to be asked by the author of this book, a colleague at London South Bank University, to write this foreword. The book *Understanding Ethics and Ethical Decision-Making* was mainly written for nursing and social work students but could also be used by professionals who need to refresh their knowledge of ethics and ethical decision-making. The value of the book could be seen from its practical approach to learning the subject of ethics. After all, nursing and social work practices are ethical practice. Most other published books on nursing and social work ethics are often laden with theories and principles, and not suitable for students, especially for those without prior ethical knowledge and going into practice placement. This book offers an excellent contribution to the understanding of the relationship between learning ethical theories and principles and their practice applications. In chapter 4 and 5 of the book, for instance, three ethical theories and four ethical principles are written in a comprehensive and readable way. Citing Rainbow (2002), the author posited that the ethical theories and principles discussed in the book are the bedrock of ethical analysis because they are the standpoints from which guidance can be obtained along the pathway to an ethical decision. In discussing the relationship between ethical theory and ethical principle, the author once again cites Rainbow (2002) and argues that each ethical theory attempts to hold fast to the ethical principles that lead to success when used in an attempt to resolve ethical dilemma. To resolve any dilemma, therefore, ethical theory must be directed towards a universal set of goals. Ethical principles are the universal goals that each theory tries to achieve in order to successfully resolve the ethical dilemma. You will be forgiven for thinking that you have read this before, but be rest assured that you will benefit immensely from the practical approach adopted by the author of this book. What is most refreshing about the book is the simplicity the author has adopted in discussing the ethical theories and principles; ethical issues and dilemmas; approaches to moral reasoning and decision-making; models for ethical analysis and decision making; and case studies and discussions to illustrate application of ethical theories and principles to practice.

In addition, the book introduces a new model for ethical analysis and decision making in chapter 8 to help students gain more confidence in dealing with ethical problems. It uses carefully selected case studies based on episodes of care involving real people and discussions to illustrate the model use in practice. The overall value of the model could be seen from its ability to help readers identify ethical problems and apply appropriate strategies to deal with the problems as well as ranging breadth of knowledge of their interpretations. This book deserves a wide audience, as it places ethics at the centre of nursing and social work practice.

Jude C. Ibe, RMN, BA (Hons) MSc. (Econs,) PGCE (FE) RNT, principal lecturer and programme leader, Department of Family Care and Mental Health, University of Greenwich, London.

Introduction

The place of ethics and ethical decision-making in nursing and social work practice cannot be overemphasized. Ethics, for example, *permeates most things nursing and social work professionals do in practice.* In other words, *nursing and social work are essentially ethical practices.* This view is reinforced by the National Association of Social Workers (2008) when it emphatically states in the preamble to its Code of Ethics that 'professional ethics are at the core of social work'. Similarly, RCN (2009) emphasises that nursing is an ethical practice. In addition, ethics provide the tools to develop essential ethical decision-making skills (Bowles *et al,* 2006). We like to add that *any successful action in life will depend on the quality of the decision made, and quality of the decision will depend on relevant knowledge.*

Thus, making successful ethical decisions to a large extent would depend on one's knowledge of ethics.

Social workers are expected to gain knowledge of ethics and ethical decision-making necessary for resolution of dilemmas and conflicts in both interpersonal and professional contexts (QAA, 2008). Similarly, nurses are expected to gain knowledge of ethics and skills for ethical decision-making that will enable them to resolve the complexities arising from ethical dilemmas in practice (NMC, 2004). Furthermore, views abound in literature, stressing the importance of ethical knowledge for both nursing and social work professionals, as they are involved in ethical decision-making to resolve many ethical dilemmas in practice (NOS, 2002; Matzo *et al,* 2004; Fry, 2008; NMC, 2008). These expectations and views influenced the title of this book, *"Understanding Ethics and Ethical Decision-Making".*

The decisions nursing and social work professionals make impact on the life of vulnerable people. For example, social workers have traditionally made decisions to intervene and protect the most vulnerable members of the society. They also decide who amongst them should receive scarce resources, whether from charitable or government sources? In addition, they make decisions to protect clients who are destitute due to homelessness or have financial problems due to unemployment(Taylor, 2010).Nurses also make decisions to protect and care for patients who are vulnerable due to ill health, who are frail due to old age, and who need care and support due to young age. In addition, they make decisions to support patients who may be worried and anxious about the future, who have a sense of helplessness or feel powerless to resolve their problems, and who may also be lacking in understanding of what is happening to them (Milberg et al, 2007).

Determining the appropriate decision to take when faced with a complex ethical dilemma concerning a vulnerable patient or client can be a challenge. As one scholar suggests, Codes of Professional Conduct gives relatively little guidance in resolving ethical dilemmas. He added that most texts on ethics are often laden with theories and principles, and discuss ethical dilemmas from multiple perspectives without specific methods on how to resolve the dilemmas, leaving the readers pondering which perspective is most likely to produce an ethical decision (Hartsell, 2006). This book introduces ethics in a gentle way by illustrating the kinds of ethical dilemma that readers may come across in nursing and social work practices and set them in context using case studies and discussions. The aim of this book is to help readers gain ethical knowledge that would help them analyse ethical issues and dilemmas and make sound ethical decisions. While the book acknowledges the importance of exploring many different points of view about ethical decision-making, it proposes a simple model for ethical decision that is easy to learn and apply in practice. The book argues that nursing and social work professionals may implement different courses of action when faced with the same ethical dilemma. This is because there is usually no single right answer to a complex ethical dilemma. However, if they follow suggestions in this book, they would be able to give a common ethical and professional justification for their decisions.

This book is mainly written for nursing and social work students but is firmly grounded in practice examples. The intention is to prepare the students to deal with ethical problems in practice placement. Thus, the book discusses, among other things, the ethical theories and principles, and uses case study discussions to demonstrate application of the ethical theories, principles, and models to practice problems. The case studies used in this book are based on episodes of care, but the names and places have been changed to maintain confidentiality in accordance with Nursing and Midwifery Council (NMC) (2008) and General Social Care Council (GSCC) (2002). Some scholars defined case studies as complex examples that give an insight into the context of a problem as well as illustrating the main point (Fry *et al*,1999). Case studies will be used in this book to describe episodes of care that illustrate conflicts arising from legal rules, values and ethical principles culminating in ethical dilemmas. The case study discussions, on the other hand, will demonstrate among other things that ethical dilemmas could be resolved by making choices between options that must be assessed on basis of right (ethical) or wrong (unethical).

In referring to social work, Taylor (2010, p.2) posited that "it is increasingly important for social workers to be able to articulate the rationale for their judgements and decisions, drawing on research evidence, theory and the use of robust assessment tools, and relating these to relevant parameters of law, policy and principles." He added that professional knowledge, values of patients or clients, nursing, and social work values, values of the organisations in which they work, and values of the society in which they live are an intrinsic part of ethical decision-making processes that must be considered in any attempt to make sound ethical decisions. Thus, this book drew from our professional knowledge of legal rules, ethical principles, and societal and professional values to help students gain knowledge and understanding relevant to ethical decision-making with all patient or client groups and in both nursing and social work settings.

Organisation of the book

Through carefully constructed chapters, the book provides details on the essential aspects of ethical knowledge that students need to work through ethical problems and make sound decisions:

We begin in Chapter 1 by examining several relevant and important themes in contemporary nursing and social work practice. These themes are ethics and branches of ethics, morals, and values. This is to help readers learn or reinforce existing knowledge of the themes.

Chapter 2 explores the main reasons given for ethics in nursing and social work education. The themes discussed include the need to meet requirements of the law, develop knowledge required for dealing with ethical dilemmas, gain knowledge of how to handle conflict that may arise in relationship with other professionals, and deal with cultural diversity of patient and client groups. The chapter will argue that ethical education is crucial to achieving the above goals.

The focus of Chapter 3 is firmly on consideration of nursing and social work as moral practice and duties to act ethically. The themes covered include duty to protect vulnerable people, duty to act as patient's or client's advocate, duty to assess potential risks and empower those in care, the need to work within ethical standards and laws, and the duty to maintain confidentiality of information within professional boundaries.

Chapter 4 explores value of the three ethical theories that prescribe morally right actions. The chapter also examines some of the major criticisms of the individual theories and discusses how they differ from each other.

Chapter 5 explores the four ethical principles and how they inform nursing and social work practice. As conflicting principles often give rise to ethical dilemma, the chapter will discuss model for screening ethical principles and use case studies and discussions to illustrate how ethical dilemma could be resolved by identifying and applying the principle or legal obligation that take precedence over others.

Chapter 6 examines the common ethical issues and dilemmas nursing and social work professionals usually face in practice. The issues discussed include conflicting moral imperative, informed consent, best interest, and giving information and equitable distribution of services and resources.

Chapter 7 clearly defines moral reasoning and discusses ethical principles, values, and legal-based approaches as basis for resolving ethical dilemmas and making decisions. The chapter also uses case study discussions to illustrate application of the approaches.

Chapter 8 discusses the values of models in ethical decision-making and proposes a simple model to aid analysis of ethical dilemmas and decision making. The chapter drew from the work of many scholars who had written on ethical decision-making models in order to develop a supportive approach that guide ethical decisions in nursing and social work practice. In addition, uses case studies and discussions to illustrate use of the model in ethical decision-making process.

A chapter summary is provided at the end of each of the eight chapters. The book concludes with a brief summary of how the aim of the book was met and areas requiring future research and publications.

Finally, one of the greatest challenges faced in writing this book is the demand to organise the content of the chapters in a sequential and logical order. We have done our best to address such demands from some of the script reviewers. As one scholar posited, it is unavoidable to write a book on ethical decision-making without linear sequence of chapters, paragraphs, and sections. This is because such books focus on topics where many dimensions and aspects influence each other in unique and complex ways. Thus, readers of such books need to be aware that there will be many interconnections between chapters and paragraphs illuminating different aspect in the process rather than clear sequential steps and logical order (Taylor, 2010).

Chapter 1

Ethics and Branches of Ethics, Morals, and Values

This chapter begins by exploring the contemporary meaning of ethics and branches of ethics, morals, and values. The chapter also explores distinctions of ethics, morals, and values as such distinctions are necessary to avoid equivocation of the concepts in ethical arguments. The distinctions are also necessary as the words are used interchangeably and different writers have used them in different senses.

What is ethics? This book traces the origin of modern ethical systems to the influence of Greek ethics particularly that of Socrates who was the first Greek philosopher to concentrate on ethics, in that, he directed philosophical enquiry into the question of how best people should live. Socrates taught Plato, who subsequently taught Aristotle. This is evident in the commonality of their work. They all taught character-based ethics in which people should achieve virtuous character to attain happiness or well-being. Corollary to this is the knowledge that ethics is based on reason, and that logical and natural reasons were required for an individual to behave virtuously (Kraut, 2010).

As one will read elsewhere in this book, nursing and social work are virtuous professions, and ethics underpins most things nurses and social workers do in practice. However, to begin exploration of the subject of ethics and its referents, it is important to state that ethics is both singular and plural noun depending on the context in which it is used. Ethics is considered a singular noun if it is used as a single branch of moral philosophy that deals with right (ethical) and wrong (unethical). It is considered plural noun if it is used in terms of quality that someone manifests, or used as a code of professional conduct (Drennan, 2003). One scholar defines ethics as a branch of moral philosophy that seeks to address issues concerning morality. He added that the nature of ethics itself includes how moral values should be determined, how moral outcome can be achieved in any given situation, how moral agency or capacity is developed, and what moral values people actually abide by (Fieser, 2009). Another scholar, Wallenmaier (2007), posited that ethics could be described as the moral way to living as human—knowing what is fair, right and wrong, and good and bad. It is about people's rights and duties, the way to live a good life. Thus, as a singular noun, this book refers to *ethics as a branch of moral philosophy that determines what is* right (ethical) and wrong (unethical). On the other hand, *ethics is used as a* plural noun in this book when it is referred to as the *quality of moral behaviour or behaviour in response to the requirement of ethical code or code of professional conduct*. This later view is in line with Thompsons (2003) definition of ethics as the study of how people behave, what they do, the reasons they give for their actions, and the rationale behind their decisions. Similarly, Hawley (2007) defined ethics as the study of people's moral behaviours. She further explains that moral behaviours could be regarded as good and correct or bad and wrong.

As noted earlier, when ethics is used as a plural noun, it often refers to ethical code or the standards of conduct adopted by professional bodies such as NMC professional codes of conduct for nurses or GSCC ethical codes of practice for social workers. The problem with ethical codes is that there is no objective, universal standard of moral value applicable to nursing and social work as each discipline takes upon itself the duty of shaping its own ethical code. Ethical codes generally are subject to change according to the biases, whims, and caprices of the professional organisation who subscribes to them, as long as the change is effected within the law. However, nursing ethics or social work ethics describe standards under which the nurses and the social workers conduct themselves when carrying out care practice. Ethics could be defined under this view: *as moral values or/and standards adopted by an organisation such as NMC and GSCC in an attempt to assist their respective members to understand the difference between what is ethical and unethical and to apply the understanding whenever they are making ethical decision.*

Finally, ethics play an important role in guiding nurses and social workers in making decisions that will benefit their patients or clients and prevent them from that which may be harmful to those in their care (Hawley, 2007). As one will read elsewhere in this book, conflict often arises in the process of achieving the goals of benefitting and preventing harm to those in their care. Such conflict often culminates in ethical dilemmas requiring them to participate in ethical decision-making processes to find solutions to the multitude of ethical dilemmas in practice (Matzo et al, 2004). Ethics from this standpoint could be defined *as the aspect of moral philosophy which helps professionals to consider what will be right (ethical) or what will be wrong (unethical) in their action and thus guide their decisions aimed at resolving an ethical dilemma in practice.*

Branches of ethics

Ethics is a requirement for nursing and social work practice as it serves as a tool for deciding any course of action. Without it, nurses' and social workers' actions would be random and aimless. They would have no means of considering what will be right (ethical) or what will be wrong (unethical) in their actions to benefit their patients and clients respectively; and would have limited guidance for decisions aimed at resolving ethical dilemmas in practice. The four main branches of ethics are applied ethics, normative ethics, meta-ethics, and descriptive ethics; each is a potential tool for analysing ethical problems and making ethical decisions. For example:

Applied ethics is the branch of ethics that consists of the analysis of specific, controversial moral issues such as abortion, genetic manipulation of foetuses, euthanasia; rights of those in care and professional responsibilities, such as acting in the best interest of patients or clients, giving information, taking consents, mandatory screening for HIV and so on. For any of these issues to be considered within the realms of applied ethics, it must be controversial in the sense that there are significant groups of people both for and against the issue at hand. The issue of palliative care, for example, is not an applied ethical issue, since everyone agrees that the dying is entitled to palliative care. By contrast, the issue of assisted suicide would be an applied ethical issue since there are significant groups of people both for and against such practice (Bosshard et al, 2008). For example, anti assisted suicide group believe it is morally wrong to help someone die, while assisted suicide supporters want it legalised as they believe that individuals do have the moral right to choose when to die (Kathleen and Herbert, 2002).

Applied ethics is mostly important in nursing and social work practice, in that, it guides a professional's daily moral decision-making. It helps professionals to identify relevant issues and ask what is right or wrong in the particular situation and attempts to provide an objective answer. It may be termed the most specific type of moral philosophy as it aims to address the problem of knowing what is right, wrong, good, and bad (Mintz, 2010). However, what is right or wrong varies from society to society. It varies from one person to another person and can also vary among different cultures, religions, nationalities, and professions. As specific type of moral philosophy, applied ethics is concerned with the basis upon which people, either in person or jointly, decides that certain actions are right or wrong, and whether one ought to do something or has a duty to do something (Rumbold, 2002). In other words, applied ethics provide basis upon which nurses and social workers could decide whether particular actions are right or wrong, either on individual or team basis. On society basis, it addresses the foundation of rules and underpins every important action that became laws in such society. Hayes (2009) citing Immanuel Kant (1724-1804) posited that an action should only be performed if it could safely become a universal law. As you will read elsewhere in this book, law governs everything that is done in nursing and social work practice.

Normative ethics looks for an ideal litmus test of reasonable behaviour. Fieser (2007) states that it provides 'The Golden Rule' of doing to other as we want them do to us. For example, since we do not want our neighbours to throw stone through our glass window, then it will be wise not to first throw stone through the neighbour's window. Based on this type of reasoning, one could theoretically determine whether any possible action is good, bad, right, or wrong. Thus, it would be wrong for nursing or social work professionals to lie, harass, victimise, assault, or abuse those in their care.

Ethics of care is part of normative branch of ethical theory which is informed by feminist thoughts influenced by the scholarly work of psychologist Carol Gilligan entitled: "A different Voice" (1982). Carol questioned the assumptions behind many of the traditional ethical theories, especially "justice based" approaches to moral discussions. She argued that justice is not the only aspect of moral reasoning to be considered and added that other factors such as compassion, caring, and other interpersonal feelings may play an important part in moral reasoning. She added that men do have the tendency to embrace an ethic of rights using quasi-legal terminology and impartial principles whilst women tend to affirm an ethic of care that focuses on responsiveness in an interconnected network of needs, care, and prevention of harm. Nel Noddings (1984), a proponent of ethics of care also sided with Gilligan (1982) by accepting that ethics of care is genuine alternatives to justice-based approaches which is more masculine. She drew an important distinction between natural caring and ethical caring to booster her view. Ethical caring, for instance, occurs when one acts caringly out of a belief that caring is the appropriate way of relating to one's patients or clients. Natural caring, on the other hand, is when one act in a caring way because one naturally cares about others. Similarly, some scholars suggest that unlike women who make more situational choices based on responsibility and commitment to others, men use more formal or universalistic approach (Fraser and Strang, 2004).

Ethics of care emphasizes that the traditional ethical theories and principles are deficient to the degree that they lack, ignore, trivialise, or demean values and virtues culturally associated with women (*Tong, and William, 2009*). According to Nagel (2005) any response base on ethics of care will be centred on the needs of an individual. In practice, for instance, a nurse may be working with a patient who is in pains and finds a particular procedure too painful or stressful and refuse to cooperate with the nurse. Good practice informed by ethics of care would lead the nurse to respond to the patient's pain or distress through "re-assurance, encouragement, and explanation" (Hugman, 2005, p. 72).

Ethics of care is also relevant to social work. It is at the core of social work values, theory and practice since social work's inception and provides a framework for making ethical decision that acknowledges the emotional commitment of the relationship between social workers and their clients (Meagher and Parton, 2004). However, ethics of care may pose some challenges which require social workers to rethink the nature of their profession in terms of better understanding of the centrality of care as a principle of social work and challenges posed by the prevailing view of morality and citizens as moral subjects. The application of ethics of care at micro-level in social work practice may lead to paternalism that sees social workers as more capable of assessing the needs of clients and parochialism that engages people in caring relationships as the most important aspect of care practice (Lloyd, 2006). Thus, social workers should engage in the ethic of care only when it is used in conjunction with knowledge of social relationships at a macro-social level.

The strength of ethics of care in nursing and social work practice is on the notion of a caring relationship, yet critics believe that such a caring relationship engenders unequal power relationship between nursing and social work professionals and those in their care. For example, Hoagland (1990), one of the most vocal critics of ethics of care, argues that Noddings' theory of ethical caring places the role of a caregiver on the one caring and the role of care receiver on the cared-for. Thus, the one caring plays a dominant role, choosing what is considered best interest for the cared-for and gives without receiving caring in return. The cared-for, on the other hand, is placed in the position of being a dependent, without control over the kind of the caring that is on offer. Hoagland (1990), therefore, maintained that such unequal relationships cannot be ethically right. This criticism, notwithstanding Noddings' (1984) theory of care, claimed universality, in that, it brings back memories of both caring and being cared for which is a common experience of all people irrespective of age, culture, gender, or beliefs. In other words, everybody would have some good experience of being cared for and/or caring for other people even if it only took place among family, friends, and well-wishers.

Meta-ethics differs remarkably from applied and normative ethics, in that, it does not concern with determining what is right or wrong but instead debates moral philosophy on an abstract level. It asks questions about the nature of morality, rather than the specifics of right or wrong. For example, meta-ethics questions whether morals as we know it exist in the world naturally or are invention of men, and if so, can they be objective (Fieser, 2007). Meta-ethics can be viewed as synonymous with analytical ethics because it concerns analytical enquiry into what is goodness, excellence, amoral, immoral, and so on (Bunnin and YU, 2004). One scholar suggests that analytical ethics examines moral claims, concepts, and theories, which involve searching for inconsistency in moral argument and lack of clarity in moral concepts. Thus, it reduces the risk of misunderstanding and promotes a rigorous approach to the subject matter (Edwards, 2009). Another scholar suggests that Meta-ethics involves examination of the language of morals and involves two prominent issues: First is *metaphysical* issues concerning whether morality exists independently of humans. That is, it involves discovering specifically whether moral values are eternal truths that exist in a 'spirit-like realm, or simply human conventions'. The second area of meta-ethics involves the psychological basis of our moral judgements and conduct, particularly questioning what motivates us to be moral (Fieser, 2007).

Meta-ethics do have some practical values in nursing and social work practice, in that, it investigates where ethical theories and principles came from; and what they mean (Frieser, 2009). The knowledge of the ethical theories and principles will be useful in terms of elucidating the meaning of ethical terms and development of principles for distinguishing between the good and bad conduct. For example, Meta-ethics asks the questions such as what does it mean to say that a decision is good or how one could know or recognise that something is ethically good. If we look at G. E. Moore's answer in his analysis of "good" in Principia Ethica (1903) cited by Baldwin (2004), he posited that "good" cannot be defined in any other terms as, for example, "brother" can be defined as "male sibling". *Good*, he argued, is a simple quality, like the colour yellow and cannot be defined in any other terms. If one does not already know what it means, one cannot explain it to anyone. In other words, unless one knows what it means to be good, one cannot uphold, for instance, ethical principle of beneficence (doing good).

Descriptive ethics concerns what a population actually believes to be right or wrong, and holds up as acceptable or condemns or punishes in law or custom (Knowledgerush, 2009). It is sometimes referred as comparative ethics because it involves comparing ethical systems, comparing the ethics of the past and present, comparing the ethics of one society against another, and comparing the ethics which people claim to follow with the actual rules of behavior that explain their conducts (Clive, 2011). This could explain why some philosophers believe that it is more properly a branch of anthropology than a branch of ethics (Bunnin and Yu, 2004). In addition, it incorporates research from the fields of anthropology, psychology, sociology, and history that explains individuals actions or believes on the subject of moral right or wrong. These different disciplines provide different types of information about morality. For example, anthropologists and sociologists often provide variety of information about how societies past and present have structured their moral values and how they expected people to behave. Psychologists, on the other hand, provide information on how individual's sense of right and wrong develops and how the individual goes about making ethical choices in real or hypothetical situations. Such scholars with penchant for descriptive ethics aim to uncover people's beliefs about such things as moral values, in which actions are right and wrong, and in which characteristics of moral agents are virtuous (Clive, 2011).

Descriptive ethics has some practical value in nursing and social work practice in that it approaches the study of morality or moral phenomena by asking different questions. For example, how does a nurse or social worker handle moral issues or resolved perceived ethical dilemmas? What influences the nurse or social worker to behave in a moral or immoral way? What is the moral believes or professional values that guide the nurse's or social worker's behaviour in making the moral choices? Answers to these kinds of questions are descriptive and could help find explanations for moral actions or moral decisions. This brought us to the question of morality. The following sections will explore the meanings and use of moral, morality, values, and professional values in nursing and social work practice.

Concept of moral and morality

The word *moral* came from Latin meaning *moralitas*, which means manner, character, or proper behaviour and has three principal meanings: The first meaning concerns descriptive usage which describes moral as a code of conduct or belief that is held to be authoritative in matters of right and wrong. Moral is created arbitrarily and defined subjectively by the individual, society, or organisation. Example of arbitrary usage of moral could be drawn from its definition by different cultures. What is acceptable as moral in one culture may be immoral in another (Hindson and Caner, 2008). The significant change of common conceptions of moral over time or in different times is an example of descriptive usage. This type of usage does not explain why any action is deemed immoral except that it has been termed as such, in most cases because of the harm such actions cause without any specific defining criteria. Actions which in themselves do not cause any harm to anybody, such as civil marriage, that may be considered immoral in some culture is termed subjective moral. The second meaning concerns normative and universal and when applied in this sense refers to an ideal code of belief and conduct, one which would be espoused in preference to other alternatives by a rational "moral" person, under specified conditions. In this "prescriptive" sense, moral value judgements such as "murder which is immoral" are made. While individuals espousing descriptive moral view would not necessarily disagree that "murder is immoral", they would nevertheless propose that murder is immoral only because we so thought (Gert, 2008).

Morality, on the other hand, is often used more narrowly to mean the moral principles of a particular tradition, group, or individual. It has come to be formally considered to be subjective concept culminating in the works of Nietzsche (1844-1900), who encouraged personal morality, and Jean-Paul Sartre (1905-1980), who encouraged individuals to make their own judgements. These scholarly works, notwithstanding, debate about the subjectivity of morality continue to feature in today's moral philosophy (Hayes, 2010). The difference between the words *moral* and *morality* as used in this book could be explained metaphorically by looking at a mirror with two sides. Morality is the one side reflecting individual moral values and principles that influence the individual's behaviour. The other side of the mirror reflects morals and principles accepted by the community as whole or professional bodies such as NMC and GSCC. Thus, this book would use the word *moral* and *morality* loosely to mean two sides to the same concept. However, morals will be particularly used to qualify behaviour, which can be regarded as right or wrong (Hawley, 2007).

The distinction of the three concepts—ethics, moral, and morality—need to be clearly explained as they are used synonymously. The distinction becomes clearer with the example considered below. Morality concerns an individual moral values and principles, which influences the individual's behaviour. Ethics, on the other hand, points to standards or codes of behaviour expected by a group to which the individual belongs. It points towards the application of morals by showing how a moral person should behave. For example, drinking of alcohol is forbidden by some religion and individuals; such religion may believe that drinking is immoral. Drinking on its own is not unethical. However, it is unethical for anyone to impose his personal morality on another person. While one is abstract in understanding, the other is defined and in the form of written code (Borade, 2010). Thus, in some ways, moral is synonymous with ethics, and as you noted earlier, moral and morality are two sides of the same concept. Value is another essential concept that has a significant influence on contemporary nursing and social work practice and thus will be explored in the following section.

Concept of values and professional values

Value is "what we believe is worthy or valuable and our values guide our actions, our judgements, our behaviour and our attitudes to others" (Quallington and Cuthbert, 2008, p. 2). "Professional values, on the other hands, are standards for action that are preferred by practitioners and professional groups, and provide a framework for evaluating behaviour" (Lin *et al*, 2010, p. 646). We define *professional values as the guiding beliefs and principles that are reinforced by ethical codes and influence what one does in nursing or social work practice*. Nursing and social work professionals make ethical decisions every day, and professional values, such as honesty, fairness, trustworthiness and integrity, guide such decisions. In other words, every decision the professionals make is driven by their professional values. We know that this is not always the case; most often professionals make decisions that are based on other people's values. This often happens when the professionals have no clear understanding of their professional values. Sometimes they are too busy and do not think through such decisions. Other times they just go with the flow because they find it easy, and before they know it, they are confronted with dilemma arising from conflict of values. This is the reason why professional bodies, such as the NMC and GSCC, give their respective members clarity on what their professional values are and what constitutes being ethical or unethical. For example, referring to social work, Parrott (2008, p. 17) posited that "the purpose of social work values is to provide common set of principles, which social workers can use and develop as a means of working in an ethical way with service users". Similarly, the purpose of nursing values is to guide the standards for nurses' actions and provide a framework for evaluating behaviours which may influence decisions they make in practice (Gerard, 2002). The Royal College of Nursing (RCN, 2003, p. 3) in defining the characteristics of nursing stated that "nursing is based on values which respect the dignity, autonomy and uniqueness of human beings, the privileged nursing patient relationship, the acceptance of personal accountability for decisions and actions. These values are expressed in written codes of ethics and supported by system of professional regulation".

In comparing ethics and values, one scholar suggested that there are two types of rules or standards in use to help teach society about right and wrong. She argued that ethics are more broadly adopted by society whilst values tend to be beliefs of organisations or groups and often tend to vary. She added that ethics are the rules of conduct recognised in respect to a particular class of human action or a particular group or culture. Values, on the other hand, are what individuals believe are right and wrong and taught through cultural or personal beliefs (Goff, 2011). In comparison, moral seems to have greater social element than value and tend to have broader acceptance. It concerns more with issues giving rise to the effect of good and bad than values. People are generally judge more on moral than on values. For example, other people could describe one as immoral for not living according to acceptable moral code or beliefs as defined by an individual, society, or organisation, but no similar word could be described by them when one is not following values. As a nursing or social work professional, people will judge you more strongly on morals than on values, yet values guide professional practice and are expressed in professional codes of practice.

Finally, value in practice will guide one's actions and behaviours and influences the ethical decisions that one may have to make. Morals will define one's character, whilst ethics stress a social system in which the morals are applied. However, moral derived from society in which one live often changes as society changes and those derived from government also changes in response to changes in law (Saini, 2010).

Summary

In summary, *ethics is a branch of moral philosophy which examines what is good (ethical) or bad (unethical) in one's decision or action*. Fieser (2009) summarised three of the four branches of ethics examined in this chapter which are as follows: *Meta-ethics* investigates where ethical principles come from and what they mean by asking the following questions: Are they merely social inventions? Do they involve more than expressions of our individual emotions? *Meta-ethics* attempts to answer these questions by focusing on the issues of universal truths i.e. the will of God, the role of reason in ethical judgements, and the meaning of ethical terms themselves. *Normative ethics* takes on a more practical task, which is to arrive at moral standards that regulate the right and wrong conducts. This may involve articulating the good habits that one should acquire, the duties that one should follow, or the consequences of one's behaviour on others. *Applied ethics,* on the other hand, concerns how a moral outcome can be achieved in a specific situation. In addition, applied ethics involves examining specific controversial issues, such as infanticide, euthanasia, and homosexuality, and the prohibition against taking human life, which are controversial with respect to capital punishment, abortion, and wars of invasion. *Descriptive ethics* is the fourth branch of ethics, yet some philosophers believe that it is more properly a branch of anthropology than a branch of ethics (Bunnin and Yu, 2004). However, it aims to uncover people's beliefs about such things as values and seeks to find which characteristics of moral agents are virtuous (Clive, 1998). This is in no doubt contrasted with other branches of ethics explained earlier.

The distinction between the three main concepts examined in this chapter—ethics, moral, and value—could be summarised as follows: Ethics points to standards or codes of behaviour expected by a group to which the individual belongs. It points towards the application of morals by showing how a moral person should behave. Unlike moral, which is externally imposed, ethics are internally defined and adopted. Ethics is often adopted mostly by professional bodies. Examples of these are social work ethics, nursing ethics, and medical ethics. Ethics could be used as generic word to refer to the best ways of behaving and living a moral life (Beauchamp and Childress, 2001). Morality, on the other hand, is often used more narrowly to mean the moral principles of a particular tradition, group, or individual. Values could be summarised as ideas, beliefs, customs, and characteristics that an individual, group of people, or society considered to be valuable. Values influence the professionals' behaviour and like ethics help the professionals to make decisions on the basis of what is right and avoid what is wrong.

Finally, we have demonstrated in this chapter that ethics, moral, and value, are not only theoretical concepts, but they also have profound impact on the practical working life of nursing and social work professionals. Thus, one is encouraged to critically analyse lessons of this chapter; how the concepts discussed are expressed in one's professional code of conduct and reflect on how they underpin nursing and social work practice in general.

In the next chapter, we propose to discuss the importance of ethics in nursing and social work education.

Chapter 2

Importance of Ethics in Nursing and Social Work Education

This chapter considers the fundamental question about the purpose of ethics in nursing and social work education. The themes that will be explored include the need to meet requirements of the law, develop knowledge required for dealing with ethical dilemmas, and gain knowledge of how to handle conflicts that may arise in relationship with other professionals and dealing with cultural diversity of patient and client groups.

Legal requirement

In the United Kingdom, ethical knowledge is a legal requirement in both nursing and social work education. For example, the Nursing and Midwifery Council (NMC) has a duty to safeguard the health and well-being of the public. The body is, therefore, required under Article 5 (2) and 15 (1) of the Nursing and Midwifery Order (2001) to set the standards of practice through education and training. The standards of education and training required for pre-registration nursing education are mandatory and have the full backing of the law under the Nursing and Midwifery Council Rules (2004) (Education, Registration and Registration Appeals). In addition, "All nurses and midwives are required to comply with the code: Standards of conduct, performance and ethics for nurses and midwives (NMC, 2008). Together with the

Guidance on professional conduct for nursing and midwifery students (NMC, 2009), the code is central to all education programmes and educators must enable students to understand, commit to and uphold it" (NMC, 2010, p. 5). Similarly, the regulation of social work education is overseen by the General Social Care Council (GSCC), established in 2002 under the *Care Standards Act (2000)*. Furthermore, a new integrated professional qualification at honours level was introduced in social work in 2003, incorporating the National Occupational Standard (NOS) for social work, the subject benchmark statement for social work, published by Quality Assurance Agency (QAA) for Higher Education in 2000, and the Department of Health (DH) *requirements for Social Work Training (2002)*, specified certain areas of knowledge that must be covered, including ethics. For example, "social work is a moral activity that requires practitioners to make and implement difficult decisions about human situations that involve the potential for benefit or harm. Social work honours degree programmes, therefore, involve the study, application and reflection upon ethical principles" (QAA, 2008, S.4.6).

The above requirements meant that nursing and social work students must learn about their respective ethical code and how it shaped their curriculum. Some scholars suggested that the knowledge of ethical code will help undergraduate students entering into practice to develop their own individual sense of ethics and be educated about ethical issues in their professional life (Carbo and Almagno, 2001). Thus, it is imperative that undergraduate nursing and social work students are taught the importance of the ethical code and subsequent guidelines that govern the profession in which they aspire to join as practicing professionals. The results of recent study on "changes in nursing student values during educational experience" demonstrated that students' professional values changed in a positive direction between the beginning of their study and their graduation. The study is evidential and supports the view that education had a positive effect on students' professional values and ethical awareness (Lin *et al*, 2010).

Finally, the ultimate goal of the ethical education should be to make students understand that ethics underpins most things they do in nursing or social work practice. Students must be able to recognise ethical problems, and they must learn and develop the necessary skills to handle the ethical problems. In addition, they should be taught the importance of professional values informed by the code of ethics. This is because by understanding their professional code of ethics and by agreeing to act according to it, they will build a strong identity as professionals (Monzon, 1999).

Dealing with ethical dilemmas

One scholar suggests that nurses frequently confront ethical dilemmas in practice, yet some of them do not feel confident in dealing with it, whilst few others distrust their skills for a systematic analysis of ethical problem that often arise in actual practice decisions (Taboada, 2004). In social work, for instance, some scholars suggest that social workers without ethical education have been unprepared to deal with ethical dilemmas. The scholars added that the social worker who lack general ability to apply ethical knowledge in their practice decision-making processes tend to rely on their gut feelings and prone to making wrong or unethical decisions (Kugelman-Jaffee, 1990; Mattison, 1994, cited in Boland, 2006). Other scholars, on the other hand, have demonstrated that social workers with ethical training had improved competence in ethical deliberation, ethical analysis, and decision making. They also demonstrated that prior education and training in ethics increased their awareness of the moral components of ethical dilemma and provided ethical framework that helped them to analyse and resolve ethical conflicts giving rise to the dilemma (Joseph and Conrad, 1989, cited in Boland, 2006; Foster et al, 1993). In other words, ethical knowledge would equip one with the tools one needs to make ethical decisions.

Some other scholars emphasised that the importance of ethical education could be seen from the need of professionals to participate in ethical decision-making processes to find solutions to the multitude of ethical dilemmas in practice (Matzo *et al*, 2004). In addition to ethical dilemmas, *the sheer numbers of ethical issues faced in practice require nursing and social work professionals to gain knowledge of ethics to help them deal with the issues.* Rumbold (2002) for instance, states that a nurse may have to deal on a day-to-day basis with patients who are not familiar with their surroundings and in a situation in which they may feel uncomfortable. In most cases, the patients are seriously ill, anxious, feel insecure, or perhaps unconscious. In some cases, a nurse will come into contact with the patients who have had a different kind of moral education, and so have developed different ways of responding to ethical problems. The ethical nature of such problem is often very complex. An ample example may arise when a nurse or a social work professional is dealing with people from different ethnic backgrounds, different sex or sexual orientation, or different religious or political affiliation. These differences require ethical decision-making skills, which differ from decision making in ordinary circumstances. This is so because the nurse or social worker needs to consider the differences and also take into account the perspective of the persons who have a different moral outlook in terms of their own beliefs and values. It is imperative, therefore, that when nursing and social work graduates leave university and upon registration with their professional bodies, they are well equipped with knowledge to deal with moral issues and dilemmas that arise most frequently in practice. Thus, the need to deal with ethical issues and dilemmas supports the case for ethical education in nursing and social work curriculum.

Relationship with Other professionals

Nursing and social work professionals work mostly in an unsupervised context and enjoy relative autonomy over their work. Thus, it is imperative for nursing or social work students to be motivated and taught how to act responsibly and ethically in their dealings with colleagues, patients, or clients and their families in practice. For example, the relationship between nurse and doctors often culminate in conflict. The most common area of conflict in their relationship is paternalistic practices. Traditionally, doctors extolled the virtues of ethical principle of beneficence often expressed through paternalistic practices, which are not compatible with nursing ethics which is based on caring relationship with patients (Tschudin, 2003). The caring relationship emphasizes respect for the patients' autonomy and maintaining their dignity by promoting choice and power over their environment.This is in total contrast with paternalistic practices where the doctors sometimes confer treatment upon patients without their consent, ostensibly by reason or under the pretext that they have limited autonomy or diminished capacity (Cody, 2003). Social workers also work on an interdisciplinary team with health-care professionals, which include doctors who often carry out paternalist practices (Cody, 2003). Social workers' role, in general, includes assessment of their clients and their families to identify their psychosocial needs, connecting them to required resources and supports that are available in the community. In providing these services, social workers make decisions which in most cases often have far-reaching consequences for the people's lives. Their clients are often among some of the most vulnerable in the society. Social workers have obligation to maintain a caring relationship, which must be sensitive and guided by transparent and understandable principles. Thus, we like to argue that *ethical knowledge would help nursing or social work professionals to decide on an appropriate method of advocating to ensure that patient or client rights and autonomy are respected in accordance with the law and ethical code.* Although ethics will not always provide answers to all problems, but in most cases, they provide acceptable justification for unpopular decision (Rumbold, 2002).

Furthermore, the conflict which may arise from doctors' paternalistic approach to care and other care professionals' need to maintain a caring relationship with their patients or clients call for educating all concern at interdisciplinary level on the ethical principles of beneficence and autonomy. Thus, encourage both working to benefit patients and respecting their autonomy. Nursing and social work education, therefore, must incorporate both values and ethics as core element. In reference to social work, Parker (2004) posits that ethical knowledge is to ensure that social workers understand the importance of ethics and values before going into practice. Some other scholars advocate for ethical knowledge in social work on the grounds that it would enable social workers in particular to find appropriate answer to the following question: Who will benefit from social work practice as a means of reflecting on the value of social work's humanitarian character and relationship with others (Clark, 2000; Feather, 2002; Bowles et al, 2006). Furthermore, both nurses and social workers are expected in practice to understand the perspectives of other professionals, their patients or clients, relevant private individuals and social groups, and moral issues that may arise as a result of therelationship with them. This means that nursing and social work students need to learn about their professional values, ethical theories, and principles, as such knowledge will help them deal with different perspectives and moral issues that may arise from the relationship with others in practice (Illingworth, 2004). These points also reinforce the importance of ethics in nursing and social work education.

Finally, if nursing and social work professionals are able to gain the knowledge of ethical principle of autonomy, they will no doubt avoid acting against their patients' or clients' autonomy (Rumbold, 2002). Thus, we support ethical education as *ethical knowledge will provide the students with the competence they need in order to act as their patients' or clients' advocate and deal with conflicts which may arise from relationship with their professional colleagues on issues of beneficence and autonomy.*

Cultural diversity of patient and client groups

Another argument for incorporating ethics in nursing and social work education stems from the view that cultural diversity of patient or client populations is changing rapidly and transforming the care delivered by nursing and social work professionals. It is imperative, therefore, that nursing and social work education programs incorporate cultural competence (Fitzpatrick, 2007). In reference to social work, for instance, Parrott (2009) argues that education in the United Kingdom needs to incorporate cultural competence in order to respond to the increasing cultural diversity of client groups. Leishman (2004) in reference to nursing argues for more practical experience of caring for patients from different cultures in view of existing lack of knowledge in relation to the diverse cultural groups and gap in nurse education and training provision across a range of healthcare areas. Gunaratnam (2007) drew attention to the complicated relationships between cultural knowledge and nursing practice and argued that such aspects of nursing are relegated to the background in current approaches to cultural competence, which emphasis gaining and application of cultural knowledge and skills by the nursing professionals.

The National Association of Social work (NASW) in response to increasingly diverse client groups developed standards that require social workers to strive to deliver culturally competent services. Accordingly, social workers must carry out their duties with regards to the values, ethics, and standards of the profession, recognising how personal and professional values may conflict with or accommodate the needs of diverse clients. They "shall have and continue to develop specialised knowledge and understanding about the history, traditions, values, family systems, and artistic expressions of major client groups that they serve" (NASW, 2001, p. 4). The Royal College of Nursing (RCN) in its foundation module for TransculturalHealth Care Practice stresses the importance of cultural education when it posited that it allows nurses to do the following:

- to find out more about other cultures and views held by people from other cultures;
- to gain knowledge and understanding of the values, beliefs, practices and problem-solving strategies of culturally and ethnically diverse patient groups;
- to gain confidence in their encounters with patients from diverse cultural background (RCN, 2009).

Unlike NASW, RCN recommended that cultural education should include aspects of demography, epidemiology, socio-economic and political factors, nutritional practices and preferences, and other information that would create understanding of variations across cultural and ethnic groups (RCN, 2009). This is an indication of the importance the organisation attached to a nursing education that embraces cultural competence in response the growing diversity of patient groups.

The term *cultural competence* has been defined as the capacity to work efficiently and successfully within patients' or clients' cultural context and values (Collins, 2005). Ludwick and Silva (2000) argue that ethical conflicts and issues occur within or among cultures when cultural or sub cultural values are in opposition. They added that certainly members of any culture hold varying degrees of commitment to the predominant values of the culture, but being in opposition to those values sets the stage for conflict. Citing Leininger (1991), they proposed improved communication between patients and nursing professionals as strategy aimed at decreasing ethical conflicts that may arise from cultural values and diversities. They maintain that lack of communication, which is more likely to occur when nurses are caring for culturally diverse patients, could lead to misunderstanding. Subsequently, the misunderstanding can lead to lack of respect for the patients whose cultural values are different from that of the nurses with potential for bringing harm to the patients.

Finally, cultural competence creates an awareness and respect for cultural diversity of patient and client groups through knowledge of other people's values and knowing what other people's value would help nursing and social work professionals to identify their patients' or clients' preferences and biases. In specific reference to social work, Abram and Moio (2009, p. 245) argue that "cultural competence is a fundamental tenet of social work education." Fitzpatrick (2007) argues for continuing education in cultural competence and shun the idea of one off course in cultural competence, or addressing cultural competence only when confronted with a patient from another culture. Similarly, Leishman (2004) argues that nursing curricula should include more knowledge and learning about cultural awareness, and nurses need more practical experience of caring for patients from diverse cultures. These views clearly make the case for cultural education. As noted earlier, lack of knowledge of *cultural diversity may lead to conflict, misunderstanding, or lack of respect for the patients or clients whose cultural values are different from that of the nurses or social workers. Cultural education could help improve communication between nurses or social workers and the culturally diverse patients or clients groups.* Improved communication on the other hand, could decrease ethical conflicts related to cultural values and diversities (Ludwick, and Silva, 2000).

Summary

Since *ethics permeates most things done in nursing and social work practice*, nursing and social work students need to develop knowledge required for dealing with ethical dilemmas, gain knowledge of how to handle conflict that may arise in the relationship with other professionals, and deliver culturally competent services to their increasingly diverse patient and client group respectively. Ethical knowledge is also a legal requirement for professional registration. We are in no doubt that these four points will convince any skeptic about the need for ethics in nursing and social work education. However, we would like to argue that *the duty to act ethically in nursing and social work practice is a more cogent reason to gain knowledge of ethics. Ethical education on the other hand, is essential if nurses and social workers want to develop capacity to act or decide in the right way (ethically) when confronted with ethical problems.* Thus, the next chapter will attempt to advance this argument.

Chapter 3

Duties of Nurses and Social Workers to Act Ethically in Practice

This chapter will focus on nursing and social work as moral practice and duties of the professionals to act ethically. The themes that will be explored include the following: nursing and social work as a moral activity aimed at creating moral goods, duties to protect vulnerable people, duties to assess potential risks to those in their care, duties to act as patients' or clients' advocate, duties to empower those in care, and duties to work within ethical standards and laws.

Moral activity to create moral goods

Nursing and social work activities, in general, are attempt to create moral goods. Moral goods, for instance, include good health, fairness and justice, joy and happiness, kindness and charity, knowledge and understanding, empathy, autonomy, freedom, virtue, and friendship (Sarvimaki, 2006). These examples of moral goods are valuable yet abstract in qualities. However, nursing and social workers are involved in creating them in practice. For example, *if one is a nurse looking after a very sick patient in order to promote her health, and if the nurse is successful and she became healthier, such action would be considered creating a moral good. Similarly, if one is a social worker and successful in helping a vulnerable client to access welfare rights, like the nurse, the social worker has created a moral good.* Rumbold (2002, p. 4), citing

Seedhouse (1988) and referring to health care in particular, stated that "health care is concerned with promoting, enhancing and maintaining health, and health is conceived as being morally good in itself. Health care is thus about attempting to create a moral good . . . health care is of its very nature a moral activity". The Benchmark Statement for the Social Work Degree, for instance, stated that "social work is a moral activity that requires practitioners to make and implement difficult decisions about human situations that involve the potential for benefit or harm" (QAA, 2008, S.4.6). These views mean that nursing and social work practice is considered as moral activity aimed at producing moral goods (Sarvimaki, 2006). Thus, moral significance of nursing and social work practice is not just a matter of promoting a patient's well-being and promoting social justice respectively; it is also a matter of the moral attitudes on the basis of which professionals carry out their tasks of creating moral goods.

In Gastmans (1999, p. 4) words, "caring as a moral attitude can be considered as a sensitive and supportive response of the nurse to the situation and circumstances of a vulnerable human being who is in need of help." In social work, for instance, the ability to act ethically is an essential aspect of the quality of the services offered to vulnerable clients (IFSW and IASSW, 2005). Thus, if successful caring for vulnerable people is tantamount to offering moral goods, nursing and social work professionals have an obligation to act ethically in carrying out the moral activities aimed at creating the moral goods. In reference to nursing, Edwards (2009) stated that every course of action taken by a nurse in practice has an inherent ethical dimension. The reason for this is that nurses' actions are directed towards ethical end. He also added that nurses come in contact with patients that are vulnerable. They have to act ethically in response to the patients' vulnerability and suffering. The following sections will explore in greater depth duties to act ethically.

Protection of vulnerable patient or client

The public would expect nursing and social work professionals to act ethically when dealing with vulnerable people due to poor health, old age fraility, care needs due to young age, destitution due to homelessness, or financial problems due to unemployment. Vulnerability may also be the result of worries and anxiety, profound sense of helplessness, lack of understanding of what is happening; and feeling of powerless to resolve problems. The position of nursing and social work professionals in relation to the vulnerable people in their care is a position of power and authority. As the decisions that they make can have far-reaching implications, they have obligation to act ethically. For example, by assessing whether those in their care are at risk from their own behaviour. The risks could be both physical such as fall and emotional such as isolation and loneliness. Thus, to ensure their safety, nursing professionals need to assess a range of risks, and such assessment requires careful consideration to the risks both to themselves and to others. The patients or clients may also be at risk from other people's actions, such as abuse, assault, bullying, or intimidation. The community as a whole may be at risk from behaviours such as from violent ex-offender or psychiatric care receiver living in the community. Some patients' or clients' with mental health problems may behave in a way that poses a risk to themselves or the public. Thus, when deciding, for instance, whether a patient with violent behaviour due to mental illness should be treated in the community, the nurse and other members of the multi-disciplinary team due have a duty to act ethically in terms of assessing the possible risks to the patient and the community. If the risks are significant, the patient could be 'sectioned' under the Mental Health Act (1983). This means that the person will be detained in a secure mental health hospital for safety and treatment. The family member, friends, or carers may be at risk from their own behaviour, such as stress culminating, in a long-time care of the patient. Thus, the nurse and other members of the multi-disciplinary team also have a responsibility to act ethically by being aware of any risk of the vulnerable patient being harmed by those caring for him or her (CTAD, 2008).

Acting as patients' or clients' advocate

The public also expects nursing and social work professionals to act ethically by supporting individuals to promote their own well-being as well as helping them to exercise their right of self-determination in making health and social care decisions. Assuming the role of an advocate on behalf of a patient or client poses both ethical and legal challenges. For example, one scholar argues that patients' right to self-determination is often a source of moral contention, as this essential right is constrained by their limited understanding of their health issues and lack of experience with the health care system. She added that for patients to enjoy true autonomy over health-care decisions, such patients must possess the information and understanding necessary to make informed choices. Otherwise, such patients will not be able to exercise the freedom of making a choice based on their own values, beliefs, and personal circumstance (MacDonald, 2007). In other words, the nurses and social workers advocating on behalf of the patient or client have an obligation under ethical principles of beneficence and respect for autonomy to assist them in obtaining and clarifying the information needed to exercise autonomy and self-determination. The ethical principles of beneficence and respect for autonomy will be discussed in depth in Chapter 5 of this book.

In referring to nursing, Grace (2001) argues that taking on the role of patients' advocate is problematic as nurses must decide whether advocating for one patient will in any way compromise the health needs of other patients in their care. Thus, nurses have a duty to act ethically in ensuring that advocating for one patient does not compromise the duty of beneficence owed to other patients. The nurses also have a duty under ethical principle of autonomy to act ethically by ensuring that advocating for an individual patient does not take over decision making for the patient. Social workers have a duty to act as their clients' advocates, as their work is based on respect for the inherent worth and dignity of all people and all rights, especially the right to self-determination. Thus, they have a moral duty to assist their client in exercising their right to make their own choices and decisions, "irrespective of their values and life choices, provided this does not threaten the rights and legitimate interests of others" (IFSW, 2005, S. 4.1.1). This mirrors their moral obligation to respect the autonomy of all their clients and acting ethically by so doing.

Finally, *given the vulnerability of most patients and clients, advocacy has been seen as having a central role in empowering those in care of nursing and social work professionals.* For example, to assist patients or clients to exercise their right of self-determination, nursing and social work professionals advocating on their behalf have a duty under ethical principle of beneficence and respect for autonomy to support them in obtaining and clarifying the information needed for empowering and exercising their right of autonomy. The next section takes a closer look at empowering patients and clients who otherwise would have had their autonomy disrespected.

Empowering patients and clients

Empowerment like advocacy involves a shift of power or emphasis towards meeting the needs and rights of patients or clients who otherwise would be marginalised or neglected (Leadbetter, 2002). The vulnerability of patients or clients meant that their rights are enshrined in many policy documents, such a Patient Charter and Community Care Charter and many UK laws. The NHS and Community Care Act (1990), for instance, place emphasis on patients' rights to choose their own health and social care provision. It encourages them to live independently in the community, rather than in institutions and hospitals. Section 4 of the Mental Capacity Act (2005) allows patients to rely on health-care professionals to act in their best interests at times of extreme vulnerability. Coby (2003) argues that beneficence is usually expressed through paternalistic approach to care by doctors culminating in treatment being carried out upon patients without their consent. However, Kennedy (2003) argues that empowering patients would completely change the paternalistic approach, which has traditionally dominated health-care practice. Thus, nurses generally have duty to act ethically by empowering their patients to enjoy independence, exercise personal choices, and maintain their dignity (NMC, 2008). Tweedale (2002) argued that, despite general acceptability of patients' empowerment, paternalism is difficult to fundamentally alter and may surface when the patients ask nursing or social work professionals to follow a course of action which is in conflict with their own perspective. It may also occur when patients choose to follow a course of action other than that recommended by the nursing professionals. *Patients could only be empowered when they make informed choices that accord with what they want not what the nursing professionals considered to be important.* The more knowledge that patients have concerning their treatment or care, the more they are likely to be empowered. In other words, patients or clients need information about their treatment or care to be empowered to make informed decisions about the different options that are available to them. However, just giving information about their treatment options may not be enough to achieve patient empowerment. The quality of the information and the context in which it is given and received will influence how far it empowers the patients. Thus, *nursing and social work professionals have a duty to act ethically by providing accurate, relevant, and timely information that would help those in their care to make informed choices about treatment or care options that are available to them.*

It is clear from the above discussion that empowerment is not only exercised within the domain of health care but also social work. Individuals who need social work services are mostly vulnerable members of the society. Social workers, therefore, work to integrate social justice and social problem-solving with personal help in order to empower people and enhance their well-being (Payne, 2007). In doing so, social workers are exercising their duty to act ethically by extolling the virtues of a caring relationship that promotes their clients' autonomy and choice. One scholar suggests that for social workers to fulfill such moral duty, they must be able to develop a competence in value-based and ethical practice that includes values as a core element of their practice (Parker, 2004). This view seems adequate to support our argument that social worker like nurses have duty to act ethically in most things they do in practice.

Work within ethical standards and laws

In this section and in indeed many other parts of this book, ethical codes, codes of practice, and professional code of conduct will be used loosely to mean the standards of conduct, performance, and the ethical duties of nursing and social work professionals (GSCC, 2002; NMC, 2010; ANA, 2011). Acting ethically requires not only application of ethical standards but also the laws governing spheres of nursing and social work practice. The rules contained in laws and guidance provided in ethical codes represents standards of conduct which society expects nurses or social workers to uphold.

According to Iacovino (2002), professional codes of ethics are the oldest form of Western ethics. The intention of ethical codes are not to replace law or morality but to regulate professional standards, define the limits of acceptable conduct, and give guidance to what kind of actions that are regarded as right or wrong in practice. *The law, on the other hand, governs whatever is done in practice.* In other words, *all nursing and social work professionals do have duty to act within their respective ethical standards and law-governing practice.* For example, the standards of conduct, performance, and ethics for nurses and midwives (NMC, 2008) require all nurses to conduct themselves and practise within an ethical framework. The NMC standards for preregistration nursing education, Draft for consultation (2010, p. 3), states that "graduate nurses and midwives must agree to accept and embrace the ethical code that all registered nurses and midwives uphold before they can enter the profession." The NMC (2010, p. 6), citing Tuning (2009) in the draft document for consultation, stated that "the nurse is a safe, caring, and competent decision maker willing to accept personal and professional accountability for his/her actions and continuous learning. The nurse practices within a statutory framework and code of ethics delivering nursing practice (care) that is appropriately based on research, evidence and critical thinking that effectively responds to the needs of individual clients (patients) and diverse populations." This means that as a nurse or a midwife, it is mandatory that one meets the standards of proficiency required for entry into the NMC register, and to maintain one's registration, one is required to practise within ethical and legal framework, thereby, reinforcing one's duty to act ethically.

Similarly, the GSCC (2002) codes of practice provide broad statements on responsibilities of both social work employers and employees. The GSCC codes of practice, like most professional ethical standards, was developed by the professional body not only to provide social workers with ethical guidance, but also to assist newly qualified or those still studying for social work qualifications to gain knowledge of ethical standards. In other words, the ethical code will assist both social work students and professionals to act ethically and promote consistent professional practice (Iacovino, 2002). For example, the duty for social workers to act ethically is expressed explicitly in the preface to International Federation of Social Workers (IFSW) and International Association of Schools of Social Work (IASSW) (2005) statement of principles which established that "ethical awareness is a fundamental part of the professional practice of social workers. Their ability and commitment to act ethically is an essential aspect of the quality of the service offered to those who use social work services." In referring to ethical awareness, Banks (2003) stated that professional codes of ethics play important educational roles as they encourage care professionals to be reflective practitioners and help to promote the development of ethical awareness. She argued that the ethical code of professional conduct is a guide for conduct and ethical decision-making, protection for clients from malpractice or abuse, the "professional status" of social work, and establishing and maintaining professional identity.

However, ethical codes seem to be too prescriptive and dogmatic thereby limit professionals' ability to use initiative and freedom of thoughts. As discussed elsewhere in this book, some scholars are advocating for virtue ethics by claiming that it provides a better approach to ethics because of the emphasis it places on professionals' character rather than on rules, principles, and laws (Beauchamp and Childless, 2001). Nevertheless, ethical codes do serve a practical function in providing direction to nursing and social work professionals. They inspire the professionals as they contain universal statements supporting professional standards required of them. In addition, it provides a means through which they maintain a common vision despite the historical and political changes and the consequent fragmentation within the profession (Banks, 2003). The professional bodies, on the other hand, ensure that the members act ethically by following their ethical code. Furthermore, the professional bodies create awareness that members should be held to account for any action that is considered unethical and are ultimately responsible for decisions taken during professional practice. Thus, *it is imperative to add here that most fundamental breaches of the ethical codes lead to a disciplinary hearing, in which the professional conduct committee can remove pin number or professional license to practise.* Finally, ethical codes that sets the standards of professional conduct and the laws' governing professional practice serve as motive to act ethically, in that, they impose moral duty to work towards meeting the standard of conduct and respect for the laws governing practice. At the same time, they serve as a deterrent for potential breach.

Acting in the best interest of patients or clients

The right of patients or clients to expect nursing and social work professionals to act in their best interests is reinforced by ethical codes. For example, NMC (2008) professional code of conduct requires nurses to promote the welfare of their patients by acting in their best interest. Similarly, the GSCC (2002, S.1) code of practice states that "as a social care worker you must protect the rights and promote the interests of service users and carers". Acting in the best interest of patient or client mirrors the ethical principle of beneficence; this will be discussed in Chapter 5. The principle requires nursing and social work professionals to promote good and act for the benefit of those in their care. The principle also reinforces utilitarian value of promoting highest good for the greatest number of people. It does seem plausible to suggest that acting in the patients' or clients' best interest supports the claim that nurses and social workers have a duty to act ethically. The utilitarian theory of ethics will be discussed in Chapter 4, and acting in the best interest of a patient or client will be discussed further in chapter 6 and 8 of this book.

Finally, the ethical principle of justice requires fair, equitable, and appropriate treatment in the light of what is due or owed to a patient or client (Beauchamp and Childress, 2001). Thus, *nursing and social work professionals, acting under the ethical principle of justice are expected to identifying what is in the patients' or clients' best interest, and acting to meet such best interest irrespective of the patients' or clients' ethnicity, religion, sexual orientation, health status, and so on.* Such act tantamount to acting ethically. However, acting in the best interest is an ethical issue which is any situation where a social worker, for instance, knows exactly what should be done both from ethical and legal perspective (Banks and Williams, 2005). Thus, *it will be plausible to argue that acting in the best interest of any patient or client is usually in response to the duty to act ethically.*

Maintaining confidentiality of information

Confidentiality is both legal and ethical concepts. The relationship between nursing and social work professionals and those in their care carries both legal and ethical duties of confidence. The legal basis of confidence could be seen from the rules contained in both Data Protection Act (1998) and Human Right Act (1998). For example, the Data Protection Act provides protection against misusing personal data, and a host of UK common laws provides judgements on the balance between the rights of the individual and the needs of the society. The Human Rights Act, on the other hand, allows those individuals and those in care to bring action in court for breach of confidence or against a public authority, such as National Health Service (NHS) or Social Service, on the basis of the convention's right to privacy under Article 8. The ethical basis for confidence, on the other hand, could be seen from a duty perspective, which is grounded in the principle of respect for autonomy. An autonomous patient's or client's rights in service include right to confidentiality, and any breach on the part of the nursing or the social work professional tantamount to disrespecting the autonomy of the patient or client.

Nursing and social work professionals have a duty to act ethically by explicitly or implicitly acting to keep confidential the information provided to them by those in their care; disclosure is only permitted within exception rules clearly defined in the above laws and ethical codes. Exception rules, for instance, include disclosure on need to know basis, disclosure in response to court order, disclosure to protect individual or community at risk, and disclosure to prevent crime or act of terrorism. The type of information may range from facts about the patients' or clients' physical well-being and financial situation to personal details about their health status and relationships. An illegal disclosure of such information can be embarrassing and worrying, and yet patients and clients talk openly to nursing and social work professionals about them trusting that they would maintain the confidentiality of such information. The professionals, on the other hand, have a duty to act ethically by ensuring that they do not breach the trust bestowed upon them and follow established guidelines and procedures laid down in law and their professional codes of conduct. For example, the Data Protection Act ensures the confidentiality of information stored on computer database is protected through control access; the Access to Health Records Act (1990) and the Access to Personal Files Act (1987) establish procedures for handling confidential data. NMC (2008) and GSCC (2002) professional codes of practice also lay down standards of confidentiality expected of their respective members. Finally, nursing and social work professionals have both moral and legal duties to confidentiality of information, as it is important, among other things, in building trust with those in their care.

Summary

This chapter has drawn attention to the duties nursing and social work professionals have to act ethically. The chapter argues that professionals have a duty to act ethically because they create moral goods, support the needs and empower vulnerable people in their care, act in the best interest of their patients or clients, maintain confidentiality of information, act to meet standard specified in their code of professional conduct, and respect the law. The fulfillment of these duties is essential if those in care of the nursing and social work professionals are to enjoy independence, exercise personal choices, and maintain their dignity.

Finally, acting ethically is about doing the right (ethical) thing and avoiding the wrong (unethical) thing. Ethical theories provide means of determining whether an action or a decision is right or wrong. Three of the main theories relevant to nursing and social work practice will be discussed in the next chapter.

Chapter 4

Ethical Theories as Prescriptions for Ethical Right Decision

Nursing and social work professionals have traditionally wrestled on daily basis with the wrongness or rightness of their decisions. Ethical theories, in general, have come to dominate the contemporary debate as to which one best provides practical answer to the question of moral right or wrong. According to Beauchamp and Childress (2001), ethical theories are philosophically rational set of propositions that attempts to offer broad norms for the guidance and evaluation of ethical decisions. They added that the value of ethical theories from this stand point is in their attempt to set out prescriptions for morally right decisions by attempting to show that ethical decisions, which accord with certain specified criteria, are ethically right or wrong. In this chapter, the values of three ethical theories that prescribe moral right decisions will be explored in relation to how nurses and social workers could utilise them in ethical decisions. This chapter will also examine some of the major criticisms of the individual theories and discuss how they differ from each other.

Consequence-Based ethics

Consequentialism is the theory underpinning consequence-based ethics. Jeremy Bentham (1748-1832) is one of the earliest proponents of utilitarian theory, which is a forerunner of consequential theory of ethics. He measured the costs and benefits of a decision or action by the amount of happiness it gave to the parties involved in the situation. Happiness is measured in terms of utility or benefit it brings, yet it is difficult to measure. Nursing and social work professionals could, for instance, try to measure how broad the smiles on the faces of those in their care are as they leave their practice setting. The broader the smile, the happier they seem to be, but how meaningful would such an expression of happiness be? Is the happiness short term or long lasting? Could happiness be measured in this way? What good is produced by the happiness? What makes one patient happy and another sad and so on? (Sweet, 2008) It is obvious from these questions that happiness is not the best measure of benefit of nursing or social care service for those in receipt of such care service. Nursing and social work professionals, therefore, need to find other ways of measuring the outcomes, benefit, or consequences of their actions (Smith, 1999). Having said that, it is imperative to point out that Bentham, a utilitarian was concerned mainly with producing the greatest happiness or the greatest good for the greatest number of people. This is obtainable in today's health and social care services when it comes to the issue of allocating resources. The decision to allocate limited health and social care resources is often taken in the best interest of majority as opposed to the best interest of an individual or minority.

Consequentialism was a term coined by Anscombe (1958) in her essay entitled *Modern Moral Philosophy*. She used the term to describe what she saw as the central error of certain moral theories, particularly those propounded by John Stuart Mill (1806-1873) and Henry Sidgwick (1838-1900). Both Mill and Sidgwick were utilitarian philosophers who shared Bentham's view that what matters is the aggregate happiness: the happiness of everyone and not the happiness of any particular person. For example, Mill (1998) proposed a hierarchy of pleasures and stated that the pursuit of certain kinds of pleasure is more highly valued than the pursuit of other pleasures. Sidgwick (1907), on the other hand, argued that a certain degree of egoism promotes general welfare for two reasons: first, because individuals know how to please themselves best, and second, if everyone were an "austere altruist," then general welfare would inevitably decrease. Anscombe's (1958) consequential theory opposed these views as she postulated that correct moral decision is determined solely by a cost and benefit analysis of a decision's consequences.

Practice value of consequence-based approach

The ethical theory of consequentialism concerns deciding what is ethical right or wrong based on the outcome of an action or decision taken. The older version of the same theory is utilitarianism, which is accredited to Jeremy Bentham and John Stuart Mill; both of whom posit that that decision can be thought of as ethically correct if it brings about greatest amount of happiness and minimise harm. The practical value of consequence-based ethics approach is that it enables nursing and social work professionals to assess any ethical situation, weighs up the pros and cons against a particular form of decision or action, and chooses and considers the outcomes (consequences) that offer greater benefit and less harm to those in their care. In other words, it enables the professionals to determine ethical responsibility by weighing the penalty of their decisions or actions (Smith, 1999). For example, to make ethical right decision under this theory, first one needs to establish both the good and bad consequences of the decision. Second, one needs to determine whether the total good consequences of the decision outweigh the total bad consequences. If the good consequences are greater, then the decision is ethically right. If the bad consequences are greater, then the decision is ethically wrong (Fieser, 2009). Some scholars believe that the value placed on the decision in terms of right or wrong will depend on the good or bad consequences resulting from such decision (Beauchamp and Childress, 2001). This means that a decision is right if it produces the best overall result. In other words, an ethically right decision is one that produces a good consequence or outcome.

Finally, *the ethical theory of consequentialism requires nursing and social work professionals to work in a way that provides the greater good or benefit for the greatest number of those in their care.* According to Fry and Johnson (2008), an action or decision is right if it yields good results. Thus, a decision or an action in nursing and social work practice will be ethically right if it brings greatest value, such as an improvement in the patients' condition, whether such decision or action causes harm or not; it is right as long as it will benefit the patient more and less harm. This conforms to the requirement of Nurses and Midwifery Council, United Kingdom, stipulating that nurses and midwifes should work in the best interest of their patients (NMC, 2008). The theory also reinforces GSCC (2002) statement to the effect that as a social worker, one must protect the rights and promote the interests of clients and their carers.

Criticisms of consequence-based ethics

The main criticisms of consequential theory of ethics centred on deciding what is ethically right or wrong based on the outcome of an action or decision taken. For example, Anscombe (1958) who first coined the term consequentialism happens to be one of its most contemporary critics of the theory on the grounds that the theory does not provide guidance in what one ought to do, since the rightness or wrongness of an action is determined based on the consequences it produces. The ethical theory utilitarianism, which is the older version of consequentialism, concerns the problem of balancing the happiness of few with the happiness of many. Testing a new drug to cure a deadly disease, for instance, may result in the death of few volunteers but may result in finding a cure for the disease that may have the potential to kill million of people worldwide. It would be completely moral to do this under utilitarian ethics, thereby justifying all manner of barbarous acts under the pretext of long-term results of happiness for many (Fieser, 2009).

Consequential theory of ethics, on the other hand, has been criticised as unable to adequately explain why a morally wrong decision or action is considered to be so. The critic used the story of an "obliging stranger" who agrees to be baked in an oven and claims that the rationale that any moral theory could attribute to the wrongness is absurdity as it is wrong to bake a stranger (Gass, 1957). Another scholar postulated that consequentialism is self-defeating and capable of producing worse outcomes than some other ethical theories when one attempts to apply it in practice. He added that consequentialism does not state that we should always be calculating which of the available decisions or acts leads to the most good, but instead advises us to come to a decision about what to do in whichever manner it is that will lead to the best outcome (Ord, 2005). However, Railton (1987) cited in McElreath (2006), emphasises the significance of maintaining a distinction between decision-making in practice and accounts of what makes acts or decisions right in his subjective and objective account of consequentialism. He writes: *Subjective consequentialism* is the view that whenever one faces a choice of decisions or actions, one should attempt to determine which decision or action would most promote good, and should then try to act accordingly. *Objective consequentialism* is the view that the criterion of rightness of a decision or an act is whether it in fact would most promote the good of those acts or decision available to the agent. This throws more light on the distinction between decision-making procedures, and accounts of what makes right action from consequential standpoint.

We would like to end this section with a quote from an article by Walter Sinnott-Armstrong (2006, S.7), "even if none of these arguments proves consequentialism, there still might be no adequate reason to deny consequentialism. We might have no reason either to deny consequentialism or to assert it. Consequentialism could then remain a live option even if it is not proven." Finally, while critics may argue that consequential approach is self-defeating, *we would like to argue that it is a theory that could guide nursing and social work professionals to make ethical decisions that may lead to the best outcomes or best interest of their patients or clients.* As noted earlier, nurses and social workers are expected to act in the best interest of their patients and clients, respectively (GSCC, 2002; NMC, 2008).

Duty-Based ethics

Deontology is the theory underpinning duty-based ethics. The word *deontology* is derived from the Greek word *Deon*, meaning duty. It is a theory of ethics, where one has a duty to abide by some set of moral principles, and nothing else. It is not important in this ethical system to ensure that the ends never will justify the means. If one was to do one's moral duty, then it would not matter if it had negative consequences (Smith, 1999). The most famous deontological theory is that advanced by the German philosopher, Immanuel Kant (1724-1804). He argued that to decide or act in the morally right way, one must decide or act from duty (deon) and that it is not the consequences of one's actions that make them right or wrong but one's motives when one made the decision or carried out the actions. The *ethical theory of deontology determines goodness or rightness of an action or decisions rather than the consequences of such action or decision; that is, if one follows moral rules such as 'one should do unto others as one would want done to one'.* In other words, a decision or action is right or ethical even when it produces a bad consequence as long as the decision or action is based on duty that followed moral rules governing such duty. Deontology, therefore, could be put forward as an opposing view to consequentialist theory, considered earlier.

Kant also argued that there is a more foundational principle of duty that encompasses our particular duties. It is a single, self-evident principle of reason that he calls the "categorical imperative" (Fieser, J., 2009). A categorical imperative, he argued, is fundamentally different from hypothetical imperatives that hinge on some personal desire that we have; for example, if one wants to be a nurse, one has to go to university to obtain a qualification and register to practise as nurse. By contrast, a categorical imperative simply mandates an action or decision, irrespective of one's personal desires, such as "You ought to do X."

Practice value of duty-based approach

The duty-based approach has practice value in nursing and social work. For example, as a nurse or social worker, one must always treat those in one's care with respect and dignity, and never treat them as mere means to an end. One treats patients or clients as an end whenever one's action towards them reflects their inherent value. The respect of one's patients' or clients' autonomy is morally correct since it acknowledges the inherent value of the patients or clients. In contrast, a nurse or social worker treats patients or clients as a means to an end whenever they are treated as tools to achieve something else. Stealing of patients' or clients' money, for instance, amounts to treating the patients or clients as a means to the nurse's or social worker's own happiness. Such act is both unethical and unlawful, and hence Kant in his categorical imperative suggested that 'maxim' is morally good only when it complies with universal law. Maxims, in his view, is the subjective principles of volition whilst law is an objective principle of volition (Denise *et al*, 1999). We could explore the value of this view further with another example: a decision based on ethical duty will be ethically correct even if the end or outcome is wrong as duty is the necessity of acting from respect for the law. For example, one may decide to work extra hours over the weekend in a residential home for the elderly in order to raise enough money to pay for one's summer holiday. If one treats the elderly residents as objects one needs to control in order to get the cash to pay for the holiday, one treats them as a means. In other words, one is treating the residents as things that are just around to help one get the money one needs. If, however, one treats them with respect and dignity, one is then treating them as ends in themselves. To treat the elderly residents as a means for one to get the money for one's holiday is unethical or morally wrong. They may be old and frail but are rational human beings and thus end in themselves. They deserve to be treated as intelligent and valuable individuals worthy of respect.

At an individual's own personal level, Kant's categorical imperative regulates the morality of the individual's actions. Thus, individuals taking their own life are not only breaking the law, but carrying out an immoral act of treating their own life as a means to the alleviation of their own misery. In Kant's conviction, morality of all actions can be determined by appealing to a single principle of duty (Fieser, 2009). Fry and Johnstone (2008, p. 22), citing Kant, stated that "an action or decision is right if it is done from duty standpoint." The concept of duty resonates well in practice as it explains the duties nurses and social workers owed to those in their care. In social work, for instance, self-determination and autonomy are both core values and integrated in their professional code of practice derived from the Kantian approach to ethics. As you noted earlier, the Kantian ethical duty sees every person as an end and not as a means, which in no doubt influences social workers' commitment to respecting the choice and dignity of those in their care. Ethical duty is not just owed to patients or clients but also to the wider public. For example, a nurse caring for a patient with HIV who wants to exercise duty to confidentiality of information owed to the patient may also consider duty to his or her sexual partner, and indeed others who may be at risk of contracting the infection from the patient. Kantian ethical duty imposes upon the nurse a duty to warn third parties, including professional colleagues, who may be at risk irrespective of the consequence of such action. As noted earlier, deontology ethical theory, which underpins ethical duty, requires nurses and social workers to follow the rules of their profession when making ethical decision. In other words, the theory imposes a duty upon nurses and social workers when making decision in practice to follow their professional code of practice where it would have been impossible to practise without guiding principles. This allows for reasonable deliberation that comes into play when traditional moral judgement fails in times of ethical decision-making. For example, a social worker has obligation under the GSCC (2002) code of practice to establish and maintain the trust and confidence of those in their care. However, trust and confidence could be breached to protect client or others at risk of harm. Similarly, nurses have obligation under NMC (2008) professional code of conduct to maintain confidentiality of information at their disposal. However, such information could be disclosed on grounds of 'need to know'. In other words, information about the patient's HIV status could be disclosed to others on 'need to know' basis or to protect other people at risk. The patient, on the other hand, has ethical duty as well as rights, which include doing what he or she could to protect others from risks of infection, maintain his or her own health, and disclose accurate information, which would facilitate adequate care.

The duty of the nurse to breach trust and confidence to protect other people at risk of infection mirror utilitarian value of greater happiness to many people. Utilitarian ethicists would regard such an act as right and ethical yet the most critics of deontology came from utilitarian tradition. Mill (1958), for instance, rejects the Kantian inclination to separate morality and happiness. For Mill's utilitarianism, happiness is morality, including both physical and intellectual pleasures, in the absence of pain. He argued that the development of happiness is the highest moral goal. The view of deontologists that one must always follow moral rules, even when the decision is likely to produce negative outcome and utilitarian view that one must always seek greatest good for greatest number of people could be further explained using the following illustration: Supposing you are in a small plane with less fuel to land safely on the ground with six of your friends, including the plane's captain. The captain asks you at gunpoint to push out of the plane one of your friends to reduce weight and save fuel as the only means of saving the plane from crashing. You have no doubts about the veracity of the captain's threat. You believe fully that he will do as he says if you fail to carry out his order. You, therefore, have two options. The first option is to push out one of your friends to certain death. The other option is to do nothing and allow the captain to shoot you. If you apply utilitarianism principles, you will most likely push out one of your friends to a certain death because it would have the most beneficial outcome. Application of deontologist's principles, on the other hand, would most likely require you not to kill anybody because killing another person is wrong as a universal moral truth.

Utilitarian ethicists would contend that deontology leads to morally untenable outcomes, such as in the example above. They would further contend that the outcome of one's death is much desirable than six. Thus, you should always look to the ends rather than the means to determine whether an act is ethical or not. Deontologists could argue against utilitarian view by saying that "ends" are illusory and impossible to predict the outcomes of one's actions with absolute certainty. Deontologists could also argue that one can only be liable for one's own actions and not the actions of other people. Thus, in the example above, you are only liable for your decision whether to kill one of your friends or not. The captain is the one making the unethical choice to kill somebody.

Utilitarian approach, therefore, devolves into dangerous moral relativism as it provides grounds to justify heinous acts of killing one of one's friends to save the lives of the others. As one will read from the following section, deontology theory of ethics has been criticised for not allowing greater good.

Criticisms of duty-based ethics

As noted earlier, proponents of deontological theory relied on its notion that one must always follow moral rules, even when the action is likely to produce negative outcome. Application of the theory tends to make actions or decisions difficult by not allowing greater good at the expense of most often minimal or negative outcome. For example, it will be immoral under the theory to continue testing drugs on animals considering the pains and suffering the test animals had to go through; even when doing so would result in the production of safe drugs that would save lives and alleviate suffering of millions of people all over the world. As noted earlier, proponents of deontological theory of ethics would argue for ones duty not to harm the test animals.

The set of rigid rules under Kantian ethical duty tells what one is allowed to do, and what one is not allowed to do. Irrespective of the consequences, one is to follow the moral precepts because they are inherently assumed to be true, and they are binding upon one as a moral person and indeed reasonable human beings. It does not take into account the consequence of one's actions or decisions because of the approach's inability to take account of the individuals involved and their feelings or emotions, which are also part of human nature. For example, if one is always truthful as required by Kantian rigid rules, there will be times in one's practice when one will be torn between what to say or what not to say to one's patients or clients. To tell the patients or clients the truth may cause a lot of harm to them. If one opts not to tell the truth, the consequence may be less harmful to them compared to the sanction one will have to suffer for going against one's professional code of conduct (Smith, 1999).

Finally, both consequentialist and deontological approaches to ethical analysis had been criticised by aretaic theorists. The word *aretaic* is derived from the ancient Greek word *Arête*, which means virtue or excellence. Aretaic is a modern movement within moral philosophy, which often maintains that neither consequences nor duties should be the focal point of ethical theory. In opposition to moral rules or consequences, it emphasises character, excellence in human endeavour, or virtue. Anscombe (1997), in her paper *Modern Moral Philosophy*, implicitly discussed 'aretaic' when she criticised both deontology and utilitarianism and favoured Aristotelian virtue theory of ethics. She wrote that there are"no reasonable sense outside a legal conception of ethics; the present-day ethicists are not going to maintain such a conception; and you can do ethics without it, as is shown by the example of Aristotle. It would be a great improvement if, instead of 'morally wrong', one always named a genus such as 'untruthful', 'unchaste', 'unjust'" (Anscombe, 1997: pp. 33-34). We shall now discuss virtue-based ethics, which is the subject of the following section.

Virtue-Based ethics

The ethical theory of virtue underpins virtue-based ethics pioneered by Aristotle 384 BC—322 BC who was an ancient Greek philosopher. He sought to describe the characteristics of a virtuous person. His first systematic description of virtue ethics was written down in his famous work "Nichomachean Ethics" (see "Aristotle *Nicomachean Ethics*"), translated by Christopher Rowe (2002). He postulated that people should act in accordance with the range of characteristics, which formed the bedrock of virtue. The virtue ethical theory defines a person according to his character as opposed to an action that may deviate from his normal behaviour. In other words, virtue ethics takes one's morals, reputation, and motivation into account when rating an unusual and irregular behaviour that is considered unethical.

Nursing and social work are virtuous professions, and as one will read later, the value of knowledge of virtue in practice cannot be overemphasized. The knowledge of virtue makes significant contribution toones understanding of morality and stresses the central role played by motives in moral questions. A virtuous nurse or social worker acts or decides from some kind of motivation. It is important to stress at this juncture that certain virtues are necessary for correct moral decisions, and correct moral decisions require correct motives (Clive, 2011). None of the other ethical theories discussed earlier require motives to play a role in our evaluation of moral decisions. Virtue ethical theory is explicitly contrasted with the other dominant ethical theories, which focuses on principles for actions. *Deontology and consequential theories of ethics, for instance, attempt to provide guiding principles for actions that allow one to decide how to behave in any given situation, whilst virtue theory of ethics focuses on the motive which prompts the action.*

The theory of virtue approach is an attractive proposition for nursing and social work professionals. According to Cline (2009), once the professionals are successful in answering the questions as to the sort of person they want to be, arriving at the correct moral decisions will come naturally. He identified the key questions that the virtue ethicist would ask, which are as follows:

- What sort of person does one want to be?
- What virtues are characteristic of the person one want to be?
- What actions will cultivate the virtues one want to possess?
- What actions will be characteristic of the sort of person one want to be?

These sort of questions would help discern the right sort of character a virtuous person should have. This is not so with the other ethical theories; they share in common the difficulty in dealing with problematical calculations over what moral actions to take or which moral duties to emphasize. As noted earlier, virtue theory focuses on the motive that prompts the action or decision and most relevant areas to nursing and social work practice. For example, a nursing or social work professional who behaves in a virtuous manner by exercising patience, honesty, and being trustworthy in dealing with ethical problems would be considered motivated by good character. If the professional does not act in a virtuous manner, for instance, by betraying the trust of his patient or client, then his or her action would be wrong or unethical (Thompson *et al*, 2006).

Practice value of virtue-based approach

The knowledge of ethical theory of virtue has practical value in nursing and social work practice. For example, Aristotle's discussion of virtue centres on good character, which is a quality that makes one a good member of his profession. He often refers to a good moral character as human excellence (Aristotle, 2002). Thus, it will be useful to consider excellence as defining features of one's professional character (Timpe, 2007). In other words, it is the excellent character of nurses and social workers that enable them to fulfill their moral obligations to their patients and clients. Along this line of reasoning, excellent nurses or social workers would always fulfill their functional and moral obligations to those in their care. For example, virtue in nursing and social work practice defines excellent character, such as, honesty, integrity, caring, or rightful outcome in a moral situation as opposed to wrongful act or decision brought about by wickedness, dishonesty, or being inconsiderate.

Traditionally, virtue ethics has been applied to the analysis of the ethical problems by various professionals. Professional activities, on the other hand, have been argued to be guided by virtue. McBeath and Webb (2002, p. 1033), for instance, made a case for the superiority of virtue ethics in professional social work, when they stated that 'a virtue ethics for social work would bring back to the centre of debate the importance of the individual social worker, not in terms of his or her role, but in terms of character.' In further reference to social work, McBeath and Webb (2001) posited that the role of the virtuous social worker is shown to be one that necessitates appropriate application of intellectual and practical virtues such as justice, reflection, perception, judgement, bravery, prudence, liberality, and temperance. They summed up with a core proposition that for social work practice and education, to fit an unpredictable, non-linear world, it should develop means by which professionals will nurture the above virtues. And by so doing would reflexively enhance social work practice in general. One scholar, in reference to nursing, suggests that nurses who exercise virtuous characters, such as compassion, using judgement, using moral wisdom, and understanding, which include moral perception, moral sensitivity, and moral imagination, help to sustain the practice of nursing (Armstrong, 2006). Another scholar stated that virtue ethics as an approach, which concerns the character of a person, might provide a more holistic analysis of moral dilemmas in nursing and might assist a more flexible and creative solutions when combined with other theories of moral decision-making (Arries, 2005).

Furthermore, the ethical virtues, such as honesty, fairness, and impartiality, are valuable to nursing and social work practice because of the goals they serve. Virtue ethics serves the goal of offering professionals a model of good character that they must obey in order to be moral and provides a better approach to ethics because it puts to prominence a nurse's or social worker's character rather than on rules, principles, and laws (Beauchamp and Childless, 2001). You can imagine, for example, working with other professionals in a team where lying to patients or clients is seen as a virtue. All members of the team will lie to each other and those in their care as much as possible. Such team cannot survive for long as lying destroys and compromises quality of care. In addition, lying will lead to the patients' or clients' distrust of the team members, and no one colleague can trust another's promises or duty to act ethically. Lying, therefore, should be avoided like a plague as it is not a virtue, but a vice.

A virtuous nurse or social worker is one who has developed good character, cultivated through habit. This is a truism as to become a charitable person; one must get into the habit of being generous. To become a caring person, one needs to practise looking after the needy and the most vulnerable people. Finally, while virtue ethics tells one what it means to be virtuous, the nature of the theory makes it almost impossible to determine how to apply it in actual situations. As you will read in the following section, the nature of the theory attracted many criticisms.

Criticisms of virtue-based ethics

One of the criticisms of ethical theory of virtue is the following question: What is the "right" sort of character a person required to have? Majority of virtue theorists have treated the answer to this question as self-evident. However, one scholar suggested that one man's virtue may be another man's vice and vice versa (Cline, 2009). Corollary to this criticism is the difficulties involved with establishing the nature of the virtues. What constitutes virtue depends on different people, cultures, and societies. Different cultures seem to provide different models of moral virtue, and there may be several, some conflicting, within a given culture. For example, the ancient Greeks had a place for the virtue of pride (an appropriate sense of one's honour), while medieval Christian monks consider humility as the most important virtue. The ancient Greeks had an ethical ideal of seriousness, which could be articulated in religious or philosophical activity. However, early modern thinkers recognise a virtue of industriousness, which tends to be articulated in activity related to production (Garret, 2005).

The virtue-based theory has also been criticised for not considering the sort of actions that are morally allowed and those that are not allowed, but rather focuses on the sort of qualities one is expected to foster in order to become a virtuous person. For example, a person who is guilty of child abuse may simply be seen by some virtue ethicists as someone severely lacking in several important virtues, such as compassion, sympathy, and fairness, thus requiring reformation and rehabilitation. Critics of the theory may consider such immoral or unacceptable sort of actions requiring condemnation and prosecution. Hence, the theory is also criticised for lacking consideration in terms of a person's change in moral character. For example, the child 'abuser' considered earlier will still be an immoral person even after a change in character through reformation or rehabilitation. In other words, virtue ethicists may not allow second chance as it considers mainly the immediate character of the immoral actor (Rainbow, 2002).

Another common criticism of virtue ethics concerns evaluating one's enduring moral characteristics in contrast with deontological ethical theory, which emphasises duties or rules or consequentialism that emphasizes the consequences of actions. In other words, virtue ethicists are not chiefly concerned with what rule one follows or what penalty one incurs, but what kind of person one is, for example, generous or stingy, courageous or cowardly, moderate or weak-willed, or self-indulgent (Garret, 2005).

The most common criticism of virtue ethics is that it does not produce codifiable principles, expressed as the objection that it is, in principle, unable to provide action guidance. This is based on commonly held belief by utilitarian and deontological ethicists that the task of ethical theory should be to come up with a code consisting of universal rules or principles (Quinn, 2007). According to Hursthouse (2007) such universal rule or principle should have the following two important features:

1) A decision procedure for determining what the right action was in any particular case.
2) State in such terms that any non-virtuous person could comprehend and apply it properly.

Anscombe (1958) cited in Hursthouse (2007) dismissed this criticism on the grounds that it failed to recognise that a great deal of specific action guidance could be found in rules employing the virtue and vice terms such as "Do what is honest or charitable and do not do what is dishonest or uncharitable." In other words, virtue ethics does offer action guidance individuals must follow in order to be moral.

In concluding this section, it is important to acknowledge the development of agent-based approach that is a radical departure from Aristotelian virtue ethics discussed in this chapter. The non-Aristotelian form of virtue ethics is found in Slote's (2001) work. His version of virtue ethics is agent-based, which is opposed to Aristotelian agent-focused form of ethics in the sense that the moral rightness of acts or decision is based on the virtuous motives or at least does not come from bad motive and wrong if it comes from bad motive. Hursthouse (2007) suggests that the extent of the departure of agent-based from agent-focused virtue ethics has been exaggerated. Hursthouse argues that Slote (2001) maintains that well-being consists of certain "objective" goods whilst arguing that virtuous motives are not only necessary but also sufficient for well-being. Hursthouse concluded by stating that, although Slote usually discusses virtuous motives rather than virtues, it is obvious that his motives are not transitory inner states but admirable states of character, such as compassion, benevolence, and caring. Ransome (2010) suggests that both versions of virtue ethics agree that moral evaluations ought to focus on traits of character rather than on actions. They could, however, be distinguished by their divergent accounts of the ultimate source of moral value. He claimed that agent-focused virtue ethics of character are the primary focus of the ethical evaluation of action and that the source of value is not located exclusively in the virtues themselves. He added that agent-based virtue ethics maintains a radical position, in that; virtues are not only the appropriate focus of moral evaluation and that they are also the exclusive source of moral value. This book, however, focuses on Aristotelian virtue ethics that defines good character which enables nursing and social work professionals to fulfill their moral obligations. Finally, having considered the three ethical theories, their values and criticisms, let us now explore their distinction and conclude the chapter with a summary of content.

Distinction between the three ethical theories

In this chapter, attempt was made to synthesise the three ethical theories but we soon realised that this is logically impossible as they seem contradictory to each other.Thus, in this section, our attention will be focused on the distinction between the three theories and discussion of their values in ethical decision-making.

The distinction between the three ethical theories could be illustrated using a narrative base on a former bank staff that went into the bank and started shooting his former colleagues in revenge for dismissal. When the armed policemen arrived, he grabbed one of the bank customers as a human shield whilst he continued to kill people that he held as hostages. Is it better for the policemen to take a chance and kill him with his human shield to save the lifes of the remaining people held hostage in the building or to wait for negotiation or after he had finished and killed the human shield and himself? The human shield is an innocent customer and do not deserve to die and so were many bank customers and staff who were killed because the armed policemen who could have stopped the massacre were clinging to deontological ideals and focused on saving the life of one person used as shield as opposed to saving the lives of many that died. Deontology ethicist would maintain that it is wrong to kill the innocent human shield that does not need to die, even if it is necessary to save more lives. The truth is that by so doing, the policemen have allowed the killing of more innocent people. Utilitarian ethicists would argue that the right action is always the action that has the consequence of making as many people as possible happy. Thus, killing the gun man and his human shield means taking two lives to save many would fit in well withutilitarian ideal"end justifies the means" sort of situation. A virtue ethicist on the other hand, would focus less on the act of killing and instead consider what a decision to kill or not to kill the innocent human shield said about the character and moral behaviour of the policemen.

The distinction between consequential, deontological, and virtue ethics is important because when it comes to making a moral decision about whether to behave in a certain way or refrain from certain behaviour in a given situation, nurses and social workers need to be guided, and ethical theories provide necessary guide that point them in the right direction. For example, consequential theu. is outcome based, which concern morality of a decision and the consequences of the outcome. Deontological theory of ethics places emphases on following rules, and doing one's duty. The ethical theory of virtue concerns desirable characteristics, which one should have as moral or virtuous person (Athanassoulis, 2004).

The major difference between these three ethical theories tends to lie more in the way ethical dilemmas are addressed than in the ethical conclusions reached. For example, a student nurse was asked by a doctor to assist restrain an eight-year-old girl to take blood. The girl started to scream as soon as the process started and eventually withdrew her arm and the needle tore through her skin leaving a big wound. The blood was eventually taken during second attempt despite the girl's attempt to fight the nurse and the doctor off. The next time the student nurse went in to see the girl, she became distressed and refused to talk to her and other nurses. She said that she hates the student nurse for the physical abuse and wound to her arm. The student nurse felt really awful as if she had let the child down. The dilemma in the illustration arises because acting to benefit the girl conflicted with the need to protect her from harm. Some consequential ethicist may attempt to resolve the dilemma by deciding that harming the girl is morally wrong because of the negative consequences that results from harm. Other consequentialists may contend that certain harms are acceptable, such as forceful restraining of the child to take blood when the decision serves the best interest of the child. As you noted earlier, acting in the best interest of patient is reinforced by both GSCC (2002) and NMC (2008). A deontologist might argue that the decision culminating in harm is immoral and unacceptable irrespective of any potential benefit to the girl, as both the doctor and the nurse have a duty not to harm anyone. A virtue ethicist, on the other hand, would focus less on the decision that resulted in harming the girl and instead consider what motivated the decision which led to the harm in relation to the nurse's and doctor's character and their moral behaviour (Hursthouse, 2007).

Finally, the three ethical theories as noted earlier have come to dominate the contemporary debate as to which one best provides practical answer to the question of moral right or wrong and that nursing and social work professionals have traditionally wrestled on daily basis with the question whether or not their decision is right. We concur with the views of some scholars who suggested that ethical theories set out prescriptions for morally right decisions by attempting to show that ethical decisions that accord with certain specified criteria are ethically right or wrong (Beauchamp and Childress, 2001).

Summary

The summary of the ethical theories is as follows: Utilitarianism (Mill 1806-1873), Kant's duty-based moral theory (Kant, 1785-1804) and Aristotle's (384 BC-322 BC) virtue-based theory. Crudely, a utilitarian ethicist would argue that decisions are right in so far as they maximise benefits or minimise harms. This is based on the supposition that the right decision will be the one that results in the greatest happiness for the greatest number of people. And, equally crudely, the rightness or wrongness of any decision will depend upon the motives of the actor (Cullity, 2004). This is based on the supposition that there is a duty to make the 'right' decision, despite the consequences of actual penalty of such decision. The third ethical theory discussed earlier is virtue which asserts that the right action will be that preferred by a 'virtuous' person (Fieser, 2009).

Finally and in one scholar's view, the ethical theories are the foundations of ethical analysis, in that, they provide necessary guidance that would help nursing and social work professionals make difficult ethical decisions. The scholar added that the individual theory stresses different points of view capable of predicting the outcome of any decision aimed at resolving ethical dilemma and by so doing provide the framework upon which nursing and social work professionals could make decision that will resolve ethical dilemmas. The scholar further argues that to be able to achieve the goal of resolving ethical dilemmas, the ethical theory must be directed towards a set of universal goals. Ethical principles are the universal goals that each theory tries to reach in order to be successful in guiding decision making (Rainbow, 2002). Ethical principles are the subject of the detailed discussion in the next chapter.

Chapter 5

Ethical Principles and How They Inform Practice

This chapter will discuss ethical principles of respect for autonomy, beneficence, non-malficence, and justice and explore how they inform practice and guide nursing and social work professionals to make a decision that is ethically justifiable. As ethical dilemmas often arise when principles conflict, the chapter discusses a model that will help one decide which principles take precedence over others in any ethical decision-making process.

The four ethical principles, developed by Beauchamp and Childress (1994) in America in the 1970s, utilise the common moral language of almost all disciplines and applicable to ethical issues affecting most professions, including nursing and social work. The division between different professional ethics, that is, medical ethics, nursing ethics, social work ethics, and others has not helped in terms of promoting collaborative activity in care delivery (Thompson et al, 2007). However, the four ethical principles can be applied to all professional practices, thus, fulfilling the need for a move towards an inclusive and generic ethical practice. Gillon (1994) considered the principles to be prima facie, universal, and are binding unless they conflict with one another. He further emphasised that they are universal prima facie moral norms that can be intercultural and internationally acceptable (Gillon, 2003). The universality has been the strength of the four principles. Ironically, it is also the most criticised quality as protagonists dismissed the claimed universality of the principles on the ground that the principles were developed in American with common morality and therefore would mirror certain aspects of American society and may for such reason alone be unable to be transferred to other contexts and other societies (Tsai, 1999). Without entering into the debate on the principles, the main aim of this chapter is to examine each principle in the light of each serving as a useful tool for making justifiable ethical decisions. According to Iacovino (2002, p. 6) "ethical principles enable us to reach normative judgements. They guide our thinking by providing us with the basis for determining how we should act when an ethical issue arises. They do not provide definitive answers; only answers that can be justified by way of argument depending on the ethical viewpoints adopted, and the decision-making models and process employed." In line with this view, this chapter *will argue that although the principles may not necessarily provide answers to all ethical dilemmas nursing and social work professionals may face in practice but will provide them with guide to make decisions that are ethically justifiable.*

Respect for autonomy

In a literal sense, *autonomy means self-rule or self-determination. It concerns decision to allow those in care to act freely in accordance with their own choice or free will.* According to Beauchamp and Childress (2003), a person should have the right to hold his or her own views, make choices, and take actions based on personal values and beliefs. This means that patients and clients in care have the right to express themselves, make their own choices, and take actions based on their own preferences, personal values, and cultural beliefs. However, they need to be autonomous to enjoy such rights as the action of autonomous person cannot be restricted by others as long as no serious harm is inflicted on another person (Tsai, 1999). Autonomous patients or clients are those who are competent with mental capacity to make their own choices, think logically, and make decisions by acting on the basis of the decision themselves, as well as the freedom to decide how to run their own life according to their own values and aspirations (Herring, 2006). As a nurse or social worker, one has a moral obligation to respect the autonomy of those in one's care, the choices they make and actions they take based on their own personal values and beliefs. As long as they are autonomous, one is also required to respect the decisions they make about their own lives without interference (Gibbons, 2008). Respecting the autonomy of those in one's care in that way amounts to empowering them. As stated earlier citing Immanuel Kant, people should be treated as ends in themselves and never merely as means to some end. Autonomous patients or clients are liberated, equal, and rational human beings, inherently possessed absolute moral value. This unconditional worth and capacity for free will is the essential reason why their autonomy should be respected. To infringe upon the autonomy of those in care is to prevent them from pursuing their own goals and determining their own destiny; therefore, amounts to treating them merely as a means rather than an end (Tsai, 1999).

The ethical principle of autonomy is reinforced in both NMC (2008) and GSCC (2002).For example, the NMC (2008) professional codes of conduct emphasises the importance of obtaining consent and also protecting the rights of all patients to refuse treatment. Respecting one's patient's autonomy, therefore, is a moral issue in two ways: first, it concerns the welfare of one's patients and second, it involves respecting the rights of one's patients. NMC (2008) also requires that nurses should "act with integrity by being open and honest, uphold the reputation of the profession, and treat individuals with dignity and respect." Similarly, GSCC (2002) codes of practice requires all social workers to promote the interest of their clients and carers, which includes respecting their views and wishes. The codes also requires social workers to support their clients' right to control their lives and make informed choices about the service they receive. Thus, respecting patients' or clients' autonomy is a good way of acknowledging them as valuable rational and self-conscious human beings capable of making their own choices (Beauchamp and Childress, 2003).

There are two different ways the principle of autonomy could inform nursing or social work practice: The first concerns the paternalistic approach which places patients' or clients' best interests over their wishes. Rose (1995) considered what best interests are and contends that from time to time it may be necessary to cause short-term harm, such as painful treatment in order to achieve long-term good, such as lasting cure for an illness. The short-term harm following the above example is to encourage the dying person to take the prescribed medication. Nowadays, such an action would be regarded as unacceptable and 'paternalistic'. 'Paternalism' has a distinct meaning in health care. It describes the actions of a nurse or any other health-care professional who overrides or does not seek the wishes of autonomous patients thereby disrespecting their autonomy. Humber and Almeder (2001) contended that paternalism is an intrusion of a person's freedom under the pretext that it is for the good or happiness of the person. *Health and social care professionals more often than not believe that they are better able to decide what is in patients' or clients' best interests even when they are autonomous persons. The intention of health and social care professionals to be paternalistic is often in good faith but is ethically unacceptable because it usurps their patients' or clients' rights to make autonomous decisions that is driven by their own values and beliefs.* According to Beauchamp and Childress (2001), respect for autonomy requires individual liberty to determine their own actions according to their chosen plan. Thus, paternalistic action is an affront to individuals' liberty to decide their own fate and abhorrent in nursing and social work practice as it has the potential to cause the patients or clients harm rather than beneficence. Nursing and social work professionals' primary duty centres on the welfare of their patients and clients. As you noted in Chapter 3 of this book, they have a duty to protect vulnerable people in their care by promoting, advocating, and striving to protect the health, safety, and rights of their patient or client (GSCC, 2002; NMC, 2008). For example, the advocacy role of a nurse or social worker involves supporting patients or clients in whatever decision they make. In other words, the advocacy role of a nurse or social worker enables autonomy of patients or clients who might otherwise not be fully autonomous, either through lack of understanding, inability to articulate their wishes, or unable to manage their situation effectively themselves to be respected (Smith, 1999).

The second application of ethical principle of respect for autonomy in nursing and social work practice is the liberation approach, which prioritises the patients' or clients' wishes over their best interests. In practice, this involves discussing proposed treatment or social care service with the patients or clients, respectively, in an open and honest way, allowing them to make their own choices about what treatment or care service they should receive (Hendricks, 2004). Thus, *allowing patients and clients to have control over their own life would lead to improvement in their quality of life because they have chosen the path of life with the greatest amount of personal beneficence.* Although this approach takes cognisance of the patients' and clients' desires, it does not prevent them from making decisions that may be more harmful than beneficial. The Department of Health (2004) reinforced the former point when they stated that the last few decades have noticed a significant drive towards patients or clients centred care and subsequent shift in decision making from care professionals to autonomous patients or clients.

As noted earlier, autonomy is the principle that addresses the concept of ones patients' or clients' independence, freedom of choice, and action. Thus, one has responsibility under the ethical principle to take decisions, which would encourage the patients or clients, when appropriate, to make their own decisions and to act on their own values. To achieve the goal of ones patients' or clients' autonomy, one needs to decide on how to help them understand how their decisions and their values may impact on themselves and others. One must also decide on what will be in their best interest whenever they are unable to make sound or rational decisions (MCA, 2005).

Finally, if patients or clients are to act with genuine autonomy, there is need to recognise their rights to self-rule or self-governance and their need to act freely, with understanding and without coercion (Beauchamp and Childress, 2001). The ethical principle of respect for autonomy "is an extension of the ethical principle of beneficence because a person who is independent usually prefers to have control over his or her life experiences in order to obtain the lifestyle that he or she enjoys" (Alavudeen *et al*, 2008, S.2.9). Let us now explore the ethical principle of beneficence.

Beneficence

The ethical principle of beneficence places a moral obligation upon one to do what is considered good and prevent harm to others. The principle mirrors acting in the best interest of one's patient or client discussed earlier. In the words of Beauchamp and Childress (2001, p.

166), "the principle of beneficence refers to a moral obligation to act for the benefit of others." It refers to decisions taken for the benefit of others, and is closely associated with mercy, kindness, charity, altruism, love, benevolence, empathy, understanding, and humanity (Tsai, 1999). According to Galbraith *et al* (2007) the principle relates to the conduct that aims to produce good and subsequent well-being of others.

The principle informs practice by placing obligation on nursing and social work professionals to act in the best interest of those in their care and help them decide in situations where the benefits outweigh the risk of harm (Griffith and Tengnah, 2008). One scholar also suggests that in practice it becomes a ruling factor, which places a duty on nurses and social workers to act in the best interest of those in their care (Hendricks, 2004). This could explain why NMC (2008) and GSCC (2002) require their members to promote the welfare of those in their care by acting in their best interest. Best interest requires that a nurse or a social worker must decide the highest net benefit among the obtainable options, assigning different weights to the interests the patient or client has in each option, and discounting, or subtracting inherent risks or costs (Beauchamp and Childress, 2001). This may result in ethical dilemmas for the nurses or social workers as they have to weigh the benefit of acting in the best interests of their patients or clients against the disadvantages of failing to respect the patients' or the clients' autonomy. For example, ethical dilemmas may arise when nursing and social care professionals decide what is and what is not in the best interest of those in their care in order to achieve the greatest benefit. In addition, acting according to the ethical principle of beneficence in nursing or social work practice may conflict with the need to respect the autonomy of those in care, thereby giving rise to ethical dilemma. To resolve such ethical dilemma, the nurse or the social worker would have to decide which principle takes precedence. As you will read elsewhere in this book, the autonomy of a competent adult patient or client must always take precedence over any other principle.

Finally, it is important to emphasize that the ethical principle of autonomy is also related to the utilitarian ethical theory discussed earlier, which states that one should attempt to generate the greatest ratio of good over evil. The practice of medicine in which the death of an individual is prevented by treatment and care is an ample example of the greatest ratio of good over evil (Alavudeen et al, 2008).

non-malficence

One scholar describes ethical principle of non-malficence as doing either harm or subjecting a patient or client to the risk of harm (Hendricks, 2004). *The ethical principle of non-malficence in our view requires that no harm should come to an individual, either inadvertently or intentionally. It requires nursing or social work professionals to protect patients or clients in their care who are vulnerable and unable to protect themselves.* Non-malficence ethical principle is often joined with beneficence to justify decisions or actions in the best interest of patients or clients. In other words, the ethical principles of beneficence and non-malficence concern doing good and preventing harm; yet one could find conflicts between the two principles in almost all areas of nursing and social work practice. The dichotomy between the non-malficence and beneficence ethical principles provides groundwork for carrying out analysis of the risk or benefit of ethical decision. An ample example of how the principles inform practice could be where a community practice nurse gave a patient going on a holiday abroad an injection to protect him against tropical diseases. The action of the nurse is beneficence to the travelling patient, yet to provide this benefit; the nurse must violate her duty of non-malficence and may harm the patient by inserting a needle through the skin, causing pain and likely adverse reaction. In other words, the nurse has taken the decision to resolve the conflict in this example by ranking beneficence above non-malficence. It may appear to readers from this example that the two principles are opposed to each other, but there is no real specific difference. This is because *preventing harm (non-malficence) results in beneficence. On the other hand, doing good (beneficence) could involve preventing harm.* In nursing practice, however, it can be tricky to act in accordance with absolute compliance with non-malficence principles. Similar to the earlier example, there are numerous medical treatments that may have harmful side effects but save or improve lives. A great many of drugs prescribed and administered on patient do have dangerous side effects but in most cases are means of elevating pains or saving life. Yet the principle of non-malficence asserts that one ought not to do evil, inflict harm, or "risk of harm" to others. However, the saving grace is that ones action, when one is providing care that reach "the standard of due care" through proper training, competent skills, and diligent practice, could be regarded as fulfilling the obligation of non-malficence (Tsai, 1999).

Finally, the current usage of ethical principles of autonomy, beneficence, and non-malficence in nursing and social work practice seem to have self-evident value. The notion that nursing and social work professionals must act not to harm those in their care would appeal to every rational persons. Equally, the idea that nursing and social work professionals must act to benefit people in their care seems convincing to most people. Similarly, as noted earlier, it is generally acceptable that patients or clients must indicate a willingness to accept the proposed treatment or care if they are autonomous to do so. The benefit culminating in the care or treatment must be dispensed fairly, so that people with similar needs and in similar circumstances will be treated with fairness (McCormick, 2008). As one will learn by reading the following section, justice in nursing and social work usually means fairness.

Justice

Gillon (1994) has interpreted the principle of justice as fair distribution of scarce resources (distributive justice), respect for people's rights (rights based justice), and respect for morally acceptable laws (legal justice). We may not follow this particular order in the discussion of ethical principle of justice. *Justice could be defined simply as moral obligation to act on the basis of fairness. It refers to the duty to treat people equitably and according their needs.* It is a common knowledge that equality is at the heart of justice, but as Aristotle argued, justice is more than mere equality as people can be treated unjustly even when they are treated equally. Justice and equity can be seen as synonymous and imply that everyone should have an opportunity to attain his or her full potential for health and other aspects of life (Alavudeen *et al,* 2008).Injustice, on the other hand, means a wrongful act or omission that denies peoples their due benefits or fails to distribute burdens fairly (Tsai, 1999). Injustice also means treating people unfavourably because of their age, health status, ethnicity, gender, disability, and so on. It also includes failure to make reasonable adjustment by an employer to accommodate people with disability. Thus, *justice demands fairness and equitable and appropriate treatment in the light of what is due or owed to persons. It includes making reasonable adjustments to allow equal access to services and facilities to all those entitled to such services and facilities.*

The principle informs practice by requiring nursing and social work professionals to carry out assessment to identify unique needs of their patients or clients and meeting the needs, irrespective of ethnicity, religion, gender, sexual orientation, or any other differences. However, application of ethical principle of justice in practice poses a challenge. The challenge arises because of conflicts which frequently develop between the four principles of ethics—autonomy, non-malfience, beneficence, and justice—which are the best-known approaches for handling ethical dilemmas and making ethical decisions since the last three decades (Beauchamp and Childress, 2001).The following section explores how one may handle conflicts arising from application of the ethical principles to practice situations.

Handling conflict arising from ethical principles

Whenever there is conflict, application of ethical principles becomes difficult, thereby prompting nursing or social work professionals to engage in ethical decision-making to determine which principle takes priority in response to the ethical problem. It might seem preferable to work through clarification and balancing of the principles with one another first and then reflect on a tentative decision based on that examination through a thoughtful application of the principle that is considered to take priority. In practice, one will be expected to demonstrate understanding of precise meaning of each principle in any particular ethical problem and then balance the principles against one another in an attempt to determine which one(s) should take precedence (Schenck, 2002). Loewenberg and Dolgoff (1992) developed a simple Ethical Principles Screen model that nursing and social work professionals could use to decide which principles or legal obligations take precedence over others in any situations where there is conflict. Their ranking of the ethical principles is illustrated below:

Table 1

Ethical Principle 1	Principle of the protection of life
Ethical Principle 2	Principle of equality and inequality
Ethical Principle 3	Principle of autonomy and freedom
Ethical Principle 4	Principle of least harm
Ethical Principle 5	Principle of quality of life
Ethical Principle 6	Principle of privacy and confidentiality
Ethical Principle 7	Principle of truthfulness and full disclosure

Loewenberg and Dolgoff (1992) in the above illustration ranked Ethical Principle 1, which is protection of life as superior to Principles 2. Principle 2, on the other hand, is ranked higher than Principles 3 through to 7. Principle 3 is equally ranked higher than Principles 4 through to 7, and so on. In making an ethical decision in any practice situation, nursing and social work professionals should first identify the relevant ethical principles and/or legal obligations that apply. If conflicts emerge, the professional should then classify them into categories, assign priority to the higher principle, and take action as suggested above. For example, the first ethical principle indicates that the protection of human life, whether that of a person in care or other persons, is a paramount obligation, and thus take precedence over all other principles. This means that nursing and social work professionals should take action or make a decision necessary to protect any patient or client at risk of death, even if other ethical or legal duties are breached in the process.

The case study below demonstrates conflict between a patient's right of autonomy and ethical principle of least harm (non-malficence). It also highlights an ethical challenge that nurses face when their patients entrust their care to surgeons, who may act paternalistically by withholding important information that could have helped them make informed choices. In such situations, the nurses often feel forced to participate without speaking out against what they perceive as breach of basic ethical principles.

Case study 1

Mr T, a ninety-four-year-old man was admitted into a local hospital suffering from cancer of the throat. The surgeon at the local hospital scheduled Mr. T for operation to remove the tumour. Mr. T was coherent and lucid on admission to the local hospital but did not regain consciousness after the operation. He was moved to the intensive treatment unit (ITU), where he died few days later with little dignity and much distress to his family and friends. The local hospital records showed that only one patient out of many that went through similar operations survived. The nurse did discuss with Mr. T the severity of his tumour and the risks of the operation. The nurse did not inform him that his chance of the operation being successful is very limited in view of the existing hospital record. However, Mr. T rather than exercise his right of autonomy pertaining to the operation, allowed the surgeon to decide for him. The surgeon on his part did not disclose or give out any information that would help Mr. T to make informed decision. The surgeon claimed that such information may harm Mr. T and saw no point as he was going to die, anyway.

Exercise: Using the Ethical Principles Screen model of Loewenberg and Dolgoff (1992), explains briefly how the surgeon should decide which ethical principles take precedence over the other as a result of the conflict between Mr. T's right of autonomy and ethical principle of non-malficence.

Case study discussion 1

Nurses do have obligation to act as their patients' advocate. However, it seems the nurse in this case study did not want to undermine the patient's trust in his surgeon and create anxiety, which would not be beneficial to Mr. T. It could also be the lack of confidence to confront the surgeon in view of the unequal power relationship that prompted the nurse to acquiesce and became an accessory to disrespecting of Mr. T's autonomy.

In fact, Mr. T was competent before the operation, and his autonomy was not respected. Application of Loewenberg and Dolgoff (1992) would have helped the surgeon decide which ethical principle take precedence over the other. For example, principle 3, (autonomy and freedom), is ranked higher than Principles 4, (least harm or non-malficence). The surgeon opted for the principle of non-malficence, whereby no harm would be done because he believed Mr. T was going to die anyway. He may have a defense by claiming that his decision was influenced by the Hippocratic injunction to "do no harm." As stated earlier, health-care professionals often act paternalistically, which involves undermining a patients' autonomy under the pretext that it is for their own good or happiness (Humber and Almeder, 2001). The surgeon in this case study acted paternalistically by withholding from Mr. T vital information about the severity of his disease and the risky nature of the intended operation under the pretext that disclosure will be harmful. The surgeon's decision tantamount to affront on Mr.T's right to decide his own fate. Such decision is abhorrence in health-care practice as it is unethical and has the potential to cause harm rather than beneficence if the patient finds out that his right of autonomy has been breached. It would have been ethical to respect Mr. T's autonomy as he was a competent adult. This may have allowed him to prepare for his own death with the greatest amount of personal beneficence. However, the following case study and discussion illustrate respect for patient's autonomy after a court ruling.

Case study 2

On 11 November 2008, *The Guardian* newspaper reported that HJ, a terminally-ill fourteen-year-old child had been living with spina bifida from the age of six months. She was on the waiting list for a heart and lung transplant but refused the heart transplant because she did not want to endure more surgery after being told of the pain and risks involved in the operation. She was also told that only 66 per cent of people will survive for one year after receiving a heart—lung transplant, and only 34 percent will survive ten years after receiving the transplant and warned that the transplant might result in her death, even if successful; the operation and recovery would be extremely painful and traumatic. She became free to go home to die "with dignity," as she preferred, rather than being subject to the surgery with which she may endure pain and suffering, with no guarantee of success. This was after the court case raised by Herefordshire Primary Care Trust was dropped.

Exercise: Consider why the court upheld the wishes of child HJ.

Case study discussion 2

This case raises important legal, ethical, and professional issues. The legal issue, for instance, raised the question of consent, that is, whether a fourteen-year-old patient under the age of majority is entitled to refuse a life-saving treatment. The Children Act (1989) states that a child means, any person under the age of eighteen years. When an incompetent child refuses treatment, persons with parental responsibility may authorise the treatment or a court may overrule the child's decision. In other words, incompetent children will be treated with consent from a person with parental responsibility (CA, 1989; GMC, 1998). Parental responsibility is defined under the Children Act (1989) (C. 41) as 'All the rights, duties, powers, responsibilities and authority which a parent has in relation to the child and the child's property'. According to the Act, the birth mother of child HJ (and father if married to the birth mother) automatically have parental responsibility and have the legal right to consent for her if she is considered incompetent. A child can consent or refuse treatment if deemed competent by a qualified clinician. The test for a competent child was set out in the case of Gillick v West Norfolk and Wisbech AHA (1986), where Court of Appeal decided that a fourteen-year-old is competent to consent to treatment.

In this case, the judgement of what was in child HJ's best interest was viewed very differently by HJ herself, and her parents on one hand, and health-care officials on the other. Her refusal of a potentially life-saving treatment and preference to go home and die with dignity clearly challenged the intelligible desire of healthcare team to save her life. One important lesson learnt from the Gillick case is that the courts are prepared under certain circumstances to accept that a child is personally competent to make a far-reaching decision about his or her treatment, even if it is uncomfortable. In other words, the right of children's voice to be heard once they are considered competent has been established in law (MacLean, 2008). However, the right to refuse or withhold life-saving treatment can be challenged under the Human Right Act (1998). For example, Article 2 of the Human Right Act (1998) established right to life and proposes that adequate and appropriate medical provision must be maintained to preserve life. The Act also states that 'everyone's' right to life shall be protected by law. This law places a duty on the health-care professionals that were caring for child HJ to carry out the transplant even when there was limited chance of saving her life. The decision to respect her right to life must be balanced with her right not to be mistreated or degrading under Article 3, of The Human Rights Act (1998). Child HJ stated that she did not want someone else's heart and refused to give consent. She saw the transplant to be degrading, especially when there was no guarantee that it would improve her life and would involve painful procedure. As she was deemed competent, any attempt to undermine or disrespect her autonomy was tantamount to breaching her right under Article 3 in view of the pains she may have suffered following the operation. If valid consent is not obtained before the transplant, any treatment which involves touching, for example, physical examination, surgery, or dressing of her wound would have amounted to battery. Battery is any non-consensual touching, and in law, a doctor can commit battery even when acting in the best interests of the patient. To avoid civil liability, the wish of a competent person must be respected and hence child HJ's wishes were respected.

The ethical issue raised by this case study covers the three main ethical theories considered in Chapter 4 and the four ethical principles reviewed in this chapter. For example, Beauchamp and Childress (2001, p. 349), citing Immanuel Kant, emphasises that 'moral worth of an individual's action depends exclusively on the moral acceptability of the rule of obligation on which the person acts.' Based on this view, the health-care professionals' actions should be led by their duty to care, which includes providing information that helped child HJ to make informed choice and respecting her autonomy as the court decreed. However, deontological theory lacks the consideration of means and the consequences of the action (Rumbold, 1999). Thus, application of consequential ethical theory will be more relevant to the case study. As noted in Chapter 4, the theory holds that actions are right or wrong according to the balance of their good and bad consequences. Application of this theory to the case study would require the health-care professionals caring for child HJ to weigh their options and choose one that would produce greatest benefit with minimum harm to her. Minimising harm to child HJ conforms to ethical principle of non-malficence. However, respecting her autonomy by accepting her refusal to have the transplant with all the attendant pain and suffering could bring more happiness to her on the grounds of a dignified death, which conforms to the ethical principles of beneficence even when it culminated in her death.

Virtue, as we noted in Chapter 4, requires that as a healthcare professional, one should be of good character (Beauchamp and Childress, 2001). In other words, health care is a virtuous profession and hence the professionals caring for child HJ extolled the virtue of honesty by explaining the possible consequences of the treatment as any false information would amount to a breach of the ethical theory of virtue. This aspect of virtue is mirrored in the NMC (2008) as all nurses are required to "be open and honest, act with integrity and uphold the reputation of their profession".

The case study clearly gives rise to ethical principle of respect for autonomy, which underpins the requirement for valid consent to treatment. Autonomy, as noted earlier in this chapter, is the ability of the individual to exercise self-determination. The principle acknowledges the right of individuals to determine how their life should be lived and to make choices that are consistent with their life's plan (Hendrick et al, 2003). Child HJ is considered autonomous as she understood the consequence of refusing the treatment. The health-care professionals caring for her have an obligation under the ethical principle of autonomy to treat her as an individual whilst respecting her right of autonomy. As noted earlier, respect for an individual's autonomy is congruent with one of the most fundamental ethical and moral principles that underpin health-care practice (Fletcher and Buka, 1999). According to Lowden (2002), individuals have right to self-determination and health-care professional have a duty to promote right of autonomy. However, the concept of autonomy becomes more complex when the patient is young, like child HJ. *The ethical principle of beneficence often seems to be the most obvious and uncontentious of all ethical principles in child care. It is obvious that most reasonable nursing or social work professionals will agree with the idea that they should try and do what will benefit a child and refrain from any actions or decisions that will bring harm to a child.* Thus, the health-care professional caring for child HJ should work to promote her welfare. This may require them to provide her with appropriate information, respecting her decision and ensuring a dignified and pain-free experience for the remaining days of her life.

The principle of non-malficence, on the other hand, means that there is a duty not to harm others or put anybody at risk (Beauchamp and Childress, 2009). The health-care professionals caring for child HJ have a duty under the ethical principle not to cause her any harm. When weighing the harms of a dignified death and a life-prolonging transplant, the professionals must consider the complexity of the procedure, which involves high risks, including, infection, side effects of immunosuppressant medications, and rejection of the transplanted organs. The professionals caring for child HJ must have also weighed the benefits of the treatment against harm to establish which is greater. Harm can be physical and/or psychological and can be done intentiona llyorunintentionally(Hendrick,2004).There are a number of ways child HJ could be harmed. She may be harmed by having her wish not to have the transplant denied. She may also be harmed by the effects of not having the transplant, such as poor quality of life, culminating in continuous ill-health. Arguably, the court upholding her wish was tantamount to withholding life-saving treatment. There are only two acceptable reasons or condition for allowing a patient to die by withholding treatment. First is when there is overwhelming evidence that the treatment will not work. Second is when autonomous patient exercises his or her legal right and refused the treatment (Beauchamp and Childress, 2009). Child HJ is an autonomous minor and had exercised her right to refuse the treatment with active support of the court.

In absence of autonomy, any of her parents with parental responsibility or doctor could have consented or refused the treatment on the basis of what constituted her best interest.There is no doubt that deciding what is in her best interest without court intervention would have been very difficult. In some cases, beneficence and non-malficence ethicalprinciplesarejoinedtogether,assometimesan intervention would have short-term harm and long-term benefit and vice versa (Hendrick, 2004). This is certainly the case with child HJ; respecting her autonomy in the short term was beneficial to her. In the long term, she suffered harm (non-malficence) from pain and subsequent death as a result of her refusaltoreceivethetreatment.Theconcept of best interests is linked to ethical principle of beneficence and implies a duty to discover if possible what child HJ would have wanted or what she is likely to consider appropriate in the context of her particular lifestyle. Thus, respecting her autonomy is an essential part of the process of determining her best interests. There is generally no conflict between beneficence and the principle of respect for autonomy. Although, child HJ is a minor, yet she is a competent patient and has exercised her right of autonomy by refusing the treatment that she objectively considered not to be in her best interests. She must have exercised her right of autonomy based on her values and beliefs concerning the situation, even when her choice would lead to harm or her death. As discussed earlier, justice refers to one's obligation to treat others equitably. As one may recall, justice demands fair, equitable, and appropriate treatment in the light of what is due or owed to persons (Beauchamp and Childress, 2001). One may also recall that injustice refers to a wrongful act or omission that denies peoples their due benefits or fails to distribute burdens fairly (Tsai, 1999). To be fair according to the demands of ethical principle of justice, every fourteen-year-old with the same condition should have the same options of treatment and if they are autonomous should be allowed to express their wish, especially now that there is a legal precedence (Gillick v West Norfolk and Wisbech Area Health Authority, 1985). This may not be possible as each case should be treated according to its own merits. In nursing and social work practice, *fairness means identifying what is in the patients' or clients' best interest and acting to meet such best interest irrespective of the patients' or clients' ethnicity, religion, sexual orientation, health status, and so on*. In this case study, one could argue that the health-care professionals caring for child HJ could have promoted the ethical principle of justice and at the same time act on her best interest by carrying out the transplant. One could base the argument on the possibility of the transplant prolonging child HJ's life, but what about her dignity and quality of life with no guarantee of improvement? Agreeing on the best interest of child HJ was obviously difficult for all interest parties (health-care professionals, child HJ, and parents). The court saved the day when it sided with child HJ and had her wish respected.

The professional dimension to this case study centred on acting in the best interest of child HJ. As noted earlier, nursing and social work professionals do have obligation to act in the best interest of those in their care. For example, NMC (2008) states that nurse have to work with others to protect and promote the health and well-being of those in their care, their families and carers, and the wider community. This means that the nurses caring for child HJ have a duty to work in accordance with her best interest. Promoting her health and well-being is of paramount importance. This may mean that treatment should proceed even when the prognosis is poor. It might be in the child's HJ best interest to proceed. However, the decision on what is in her best interest would take into account if she goes ahead with the transplant, that is, if the treatment would work and prolong her life. Equally, the transplant might not work and end her life. Other complications could set in requiring further hospital visits and putting strain on the family. Her reaction to the anti-rejection drugs could possibly cause separate medical problems and complications. Furthermore, NMC (2008) requires nurses to make the care of their patients' first concern, treating them as individuals and respecting their dignity. As a nurse, one has to think about how ones action could have direct impact upon those in one's care. Thus, one must respect and support one's patients' right to accept or decline treatment or care (NMC, 2008). This means that in the case of child HJ, the nurses caring for her should respect and support her wish as she is deemed competent. NMC (2008) also requires nurses to be their patients' advocate. This means that the nurse should speak up for child HJ, especially as she is a minor. If she is not competent, the nurses do have a duty to work with her family and others involved in her care to decide what is in her best interest. As she was deemed competent, her best interest was better served by respecting her wishes.

Finally, the power of the principle of autonomy to overrule other principles when conflict arises, as noted in the case study discussion 2 above, does not make any other principles less important. There is no clear hierarchy among the four principles at least before starting the process of specifying and balancing their individual importance in the two case studies. The four principles were explicitly discussed in the case studies as 'prima facie'. This means that until it can be shown that one should take precedence over another in a given situation, they should all be given equal place in any decision-making process (Schenck, 2002). However, the principles have been criticised by some scholars as not being a systematic method at all but rather a loose collection of principles with no structured process to help decision making (Gert et al, 1997). Citing Pellegrino and Thomasma (1993), Schenck (2002) argues that they are inadequte for problem solving. These criticisms notwithstanding, we have demonstrated in the discussions that, although the principles will not provide an exact plan on how one should act when faced with an ethical problem, they do provide a good guide that would help one to make justifiable ethical decisions. For example, the ethical principles as noted in the discussions provided both the basis for ethical analysis and guidance for most of the decisions discussed and fulfilling the duties owed to Mr. T and child HJ, thereby helping the health-care professionals to reach an ethically justifiable decisions.

Summary

In this chapter, we discussed the four ethical principles which are the common goals that each theory reviewed in Chapter 4 tries to achieve in order to be a useful tool in making correct ethical decision (Rainbow, 2002). The ethical principles are respect for autonomy, which involves respecting the decision-making capacities of autonomous persons, beneficence which concerns doing good, non-malfience involving prevention of harm, and justice which is a moral obligation to act on the basis of fairness. As one may recall, conflict frequently arises between the ethical principles, which often make it difficult to use them when trying to reach ethically correct decision. This is the reason why we propose the Ethical Principle Screen model to help one work through such difficulties and consider the principle that should take priority. In addition, we used case study discussion 1 to illustrate conflict between a patient's right of autonomy and the ethical principle of least harm (non-malfience). The aim is to demonstrate a situation where a surgeon acted paternalistically and disrespected the autonomy of a patient. Case study discussion 2, on the other hand, was used to demonstrate respect for autonomy. It is fair to say that although the example cases present challenging ethical problems, it is likely that in one's everyday care practice, one would encounter much more difficult cases. However, the knowledge of ethical principles gained in this chapter would provide the necessary tool to help one handle the difficult cases. In other words, acquaintance with the principles will help one anticipate and manage difficult ethical situations and make justifiable decisions.

The next chapter will examine common ethical issues and dilemmas nursing and social work professionals face and how they deal with them in practice.

Chapter 6

Ethical Issues and Dilemmas in Nursing and Social Work Practice

Nursing and social work professionals often face ethical problems, issues, and dilemmas in practice. In this chapter, common ethical issues and problems will be discussed. It is hoped that such discussion will help our readers to come to a better understanding of how the issues and problems could give rise to ethical dilemmas in nursing and social work practice.

Banks and Williams (2005) clearly distinguished ethical issues, ethical problems, and ethical dilemmas social workers face in practice. In their view, ethical issue is any situation where a social worker knows what could be done both from ethical and legal perspectives. An ethical problem, also in their view, is any situation where social workers find it difficult to apply moral decision even when they know what ought to be done. They argued that ethical dilemma arises when a social worker must decide between two equally undesirable alternatives, which may involve a conflict of ethical principles, and therefore the final choice will infringe one of them to some extent. They added that it is possible for an ethical problem or issue to transform into an ethical dilemma and that the transformation may mirror the social workers' recognition of their multiple moral obligations and the complexities of the ethical issues. Karr (2009) defines ethical dilemma as a problematic state of affairs that often involve an apparent mental conflict between ethical imperatives, in which to obey one would result in transgressing another. O'Malley (2009), in reference to ethical issues in nursing practice, posited that there are many ethical issues that propose two or more equally compelling courses of action that appear to be ethically right. The nurse trying to make an ethical decision may recognise that one specific course of action will uphold some ethical principles but not all of them. An ethical dilemma, therefore, may arise when the nurse cannot proceed with a course of action that upholds some of the ethical principles or values but not all. In social work, the IFSW (2005) summarised issues, which may give rise to the development of ethical dilemmas as follows, when:

- the loyalty of social workers are in the middle of conflicting interests,
- social workers function as both helpers and controllers,
- conflicts between the duty of social workers to protect the interests of the people with whom they work and societal demands for efficiency and utility,
- resources in society are limited.

These examples are subsumed in the following discussion of common issues and problems that may give rise to ethical dilemmas in nursing and social work practice:

- **Conflicting values and beliefs:** Individuals generally come into group of other people with their own set of values and beliefs that are important to them. These personal values and beliefs may include preference that may be peculiar to the individual such as religious beliefs, cultural norms and practices. Nurses or social workers do have obligation to recognise and respect the values and beliefs at all times even when they are in conflict their own values and beliefs or the organisational practice (CTAD, 1998). In other words, it is important to remember that those in care of nurses and social workers are entitled to their own set of values and beliefs, which must be respected at all times. In some cases, one may be required to seek assistance from well-qualified and trained professionals or Equality and Diversity Units in some organisations that would provide relevant information and necessary support to help one resolve any conflict that may arise from differences in values and beliefs.

- **Conflicting ethical principles:** An ethical problem may give rise to ethical dilemma when one ethical principle conflicts with another. As one noted in Chapter 5, at times two or more principles may conflict, which will prompt nursing and social work professionals to engage in ethical decision-making to determine which principle takes priority. For example, if a patient refuses a life-saving treatment or care, nursing professionals may not be able to apply the principles of autonomy and beneficence at the same time. This is because respecting the patient's autonomy means that they will not be able to fulfill the obligation to act in beneficence (doing good) for the patient (O' Malley, 2009).
- **Refusing to give consent:** Refusing to consent to a life-saving treatment is an ethical issue, which may give rise to ethical dilemma for nursing or social work professionals. For example, the duty of nurses includes maintaining the health and welfare of those in their care. Thus, it would be morally wrong to allow anybody in their care to refuse a life-saving treatment or care. However, their desire to promote what they consider to be in the best interest of those in their care cannot override their patients' autonomy. The conflict between the duty of the nurses to act in their patients' best interest and at the same time respect their autonomy ultimately gives rise to ethical dilemma.
- *Informed consent:* When examining a patient's right to refuse life-saving care, one need to look into the issue of informed consent. *For consent to be informed and valid, the patients must receive full disclosure of relevant, timely and reliable information. They must have the mental capacity to understand the information conveyed, be able to make a rational decision based on the information, and must be allowed to make the decision voluntarily and without coercion.* Respect for autonomy is the main ethical consideration underpinning informed consent. Thus, ethical dilemma may arise when determining how all of the elements are to be satisfied. For example, how autonomous can the patients be, and how to measure the level of their understanding pertaining to the information given especially when they are faced with life-threatening situation? How to justify decision to act in their best interest?

- **_Implementation of an Advance Directive(AD):_** The decisions on behalf of an incompetent patient may also give rise to ethical dilemma. _Advance directive is an advance plan written by a patient when still capable of making decisions. It is a statement explaining medical treatments the patient would not want when he or she is incompetent to make decision in future._ Such statement could be verbal or written and also called living will or advance decision to refuse treatment. The statement may also include how the patient's wishes to be cared for in future when he or she loses mental capacity. In some case the patient will include statements in the document which allows a designated person or a surrogate decision maker to carry out wishes when he or she is incapable of making a decision. If the patient wants to choose this later course of action, he or she will have to make what is called a **Lasting Power of Attorney (LPA)**. LPA in health-care has varying designated terms, which include health-care proxy, health-care declaration, and so on (Directgov, 2011). Both advance directive and power of attorney allow patients to designate a surrogate decision maker, presumably a friend or relative, to make the health-care decisions when they lose capacity to make informed decision. **Do-Not-Resuscitate (DNR)** order, on other hand, means that Cardiopulmonary Resuscitation (CPR) will not be performed if the patient became unconscious but other treatments may still be given. CPR is an emergency procedure used to support patients' circulation and breathing when their heart or breathing have stopped. Thus, whenever possible, nurses must respect the informed decisions expressed through valid advance directive, power of attorney, or DNR made by those in their care before they became incompetent (MCA, 2005). This means respecting their patients' autonomy, individuality, and self-determination and by so doing discharging their legal and ethical obligation.

However, ethical dilemmas may still arise when determining appropriate health care for patients that are not competent.

This is because the act of determining incompetence is, in itself, complex and controversial. Although, _competency is_ *the capacity to understand information given by health-care professionals and the patient having the cognitive ability or mental capacity to remember, process and communicate the information with reason* (MCA, 2005); yet, deciding when a patient lacks these abilities is difficult. For example, *a patient or client may lack mental capacity to a varying degree and be competent* to *make one decision concerning one treatment and not another.* Furthermore, there is controversy in relation to how surrogate or proxy decisions are made. The actual decision-making in practice is often complicated even when the wishes of the patient is properly communicated. Conflicts may arise because of the moral and ethical beliefs of family members who might not be in agreement with the patient's wishes. There may also be dispute over the validity of the document (AD, LPA, DNR), formality of the directive, the question of what was meant by 'quality of life', the issue of competency, appropriateness of those who witnessed signing of the document, consistency of the decision of the patient and what constitutes the best interest of the patient (Lark and Gatti, 1999).

- **Agreeing in the best interests of patients:** As indicated earlier, acting in the best interest is both professional and legal requirement. For example, both NMC (2008) and GSCC (2002) require nurses and social work professionals to act in the best interest of their patients and clients respectively. The law on the other hand, requires any act done or decision made concerning financial, health and social care needs on behalf of adults lacking capacity to be in their best interests. The law also set out what one must consider when deciding what is in the best interest of one's patient (MCA, 2005). Ellis (2006) explored the concept of acting in the patients' best interest and argued that many health-care professionals use best interest to justify their actions; yet agreeing in the best interest of patients or clients is always complicated and often gives rise to ethical dilemma. This is because acting in patient's and client's best interest may require dealing with such personal factors as pain and suffering, safety, social justice, quality of life, loss of independence, privacy, and dignity (Sacks, 2005). There may be disagreement on how much weight to give to each of these factors. Everybody involved; that is, the care professionals, the patients or clients themselves, their families and friends, the society in which they live, and so on will have their own views on what is the patient's or client's best interests. Thus, *when making decisions about the best interests of the patients or clients, it is imperative for one to reach an agreement with all of these interest parties.* This could mean careful balancing of a range of highly sensitive issues and views. It could also means balancing the needs of the patients or clients against those of others. In many cases, it is not enough for one to just consider only the best interests of the patients or clients but including that of family or community at large. This is because one's decisions can also have repercussions for their families, friends, and society as a whole. As such, before making decisions about the best course of action, one needs to assess whether the patients or clients are at risk from their own behaviour or/ and at risk from other people's actions; the family, friends or carers are at risk from their behaviour; the community as a whole is at risk from the patients' or clients' behaviours (CTAD, 1998). Finally, to resolve many problems posed by what is in the patients' or clients' best interest, parties concerned should routinely share information during best interest meetings on various treatment or care options. As one will read in the next section, giving information gives rise to ethical dilemma.

- **Giving information:** Another common ethical issue that may give rise to dilemma in nursing and social work practice is giving information (Galambos *et al*, 2006). *Nurses and social workers are given a lot of personal information by those in their care during professional practice. The information is always given in the context of a trusting relationship, whereby those in care trust that the information they have disclosed will be used in their best interests and divulged only with their consent or under exception rule clearly defined in law.* The duty to respect patients' or clients' confidentiality flows from the duty to respect their autonomy reinforced by the Data Protection Act (1998), Human Right Act (1998), NMC (2008), and GSCC (2002). In other words, nurses and social workers are legally and professionally bound to comply with legislation and their professional code of conduct on how they give out information at their disposal, yet the duty of confidentiality is not absolute.

The law and most professional codes of conduct recognise various exceptions to the duty of confidentiality, most notably when disclosure is required on need to know basis, disclosure to protect third parties, disclosure in the public interest, or as required by a court of law. These exceptions, notwithstanding ethical dilemma, may arise when nurses and social workers are deciding what information people need to know and who needs to know it. In practice, patients or clients have the right to enough information to make decisions about their treatment or social care options. For example, before signing a consent form for major surgery, a patient needs to know the pros and cons if he or she was to go ahead with the operation. The nurses have a duty to explain the operation using simple language and, if necessary, use notes and draw diagrams to help the patient's knowledge and understanding. On the other hand, the patient or client may be upset or confused should the doctor go into full details of potential risks of the operation. Thus, ethical dilemma may arise when one is deciding what, how and amount of information to give and when it comes to passing on knowledge to other people.

Nursing and social work professionals often feel that their patients' or clients' family members have a right to be in the know. Such issues are compelling and may challenge them, yet abrogation of confidentiality is only acceptable when harm to other people or to the client is likely to happen in addition to the exception rules discussed earlier.

Finally, the duty of confidentiality is owed to patient or client. Any breach will attract sanction as one is responsible for one's own decisions or indecisive actions. Thus, nursing and social work professionals should ensure that their actions or in action at least are in line with the law, values, and their professional values.

- **Balancing the need of patients or clients against that of others:** The decision of a nurse or a social worker can have repercussion not only for those in their care, but their family, friends, and society at large. Thus, as discussed earlier, even with utmost good intentions, before making decision about the best course of action one needs to assess whether the patients or clients, are at risk from their own behaviour; at risk from other peoples actions; their family, friends, or carers are at risk from their behaviour, or society as a whole is at risk from their behaviour (CTAD, 1998). Thus, *nurses and social workers have responsibility to deal with ethical dilemmas that arises when deciding how to deal with balancing the need of those in their care against those of others, especially when issue of risk arises.*

- **equitable distribution of services and resources:** Another common ethical issue which may give rise to ethical dilemma in nursing and social work practice is equitable distribution of services and resources. Since the introduction of the welfare state in 1940s, people in Britain have come to expect the right to free health and social care services at the point of delivery. However, resources today are limited at a time demand for services has been increasing at an alarming rate. The situation poses ethical concern for nursing and social work professionals and those who must decide what methods should be used to distribute services and resources to meet competing demands. Ethical dilemma may arise when trying to address many ethical questions such as the following: Is buying more equipment more important than employing more qualified nurses? Is treatment of a young person with leukemia more important than a hip replacement for an elderly person? Is it more important to remove a child in danger of abuse from natural parents into foster home, or to pay for home help for an elderly and physically disabled woman in her eighties? (CTAD, 1998)

The following case study and subsequent discussion will attempt to illustrate how ethical issues in nursing practice could give rise to ethical dilemma. The case study was culled out of independent news online of 8 January 1993. We have made specific changes to protect the innocent party and included additional information to help demonstrate relevant principles in the case study.

Case study 3:

A Jehovah's Witness died after refusing a blood transfusion following a car crash. Mr. BB, aged 69, a grandfather, was freed from the wreckage of his car after the accident on the M40 and taken to hospital in Oxford. The hospital's press spokesman said he refused a blood transfusion in accordance with his religious beliefs, although he was fully aware that his life was at risk. Apart from few occasions when he drifted in and out of consciousness, he was alert most of the time. His wife and children agreed that he should have the blood transfusion. The nurses had tried to convince him and provided him with all the necessary information to help him make informed decision, but he totally refused. It was only then that one of the nurses made a comment to Mr. BB's relatives that she did not see any reason for all the fuss about his refusal to accept the blood transfusion; he was suffering from multiple sclerosis and was going to die soon anyway. Mr. BB continued to refuse the proposed treatment and died eventually a few days later. A spokesman for Jehovah's Witnesses said that the faith did not allow transfusions because 'we feel that blood is a very special category of substance. The Bible repeatedly commands people not to take blood into their bodies and we accept that.' He said most Jehovah's Witnesses carried a card, stating their opposition to the treatment in case they became unconscious. The hospital's general manager said, 'Our policy is to respect the wishes of patients and their families in cases where they are able to make their wishes clear and hence we did not give him blood.'

The question of whether or not Jehovah's Witnesses could be forced to have transfusions was fraught with legal complications. But a British Medical Association spokeswoman said that although Jehovah's Witnesses may carry cards refusing transfusions, these were not legally binding. She added, 'Dealing with an unconscious Jehovah's Witness who cannot say for himself whether doctors can give a blood transfusion is one of the most difficult dilemmas doctors and surgeons face today.' Then it is up to the medical team to consult with friends and relations, but the final clinical decision must come from the surgeons themselves. Legal experts have suggested doctors could even be sued if they give a blood transfusion to a Jehovah's Witness who has not been able to give express permission.

Source: Independent News Online, *Friday, 8 January 1993*

Exercise: *Ethical dilemma could be defined as a situation where one is required to make a choice between competing options that must be assessed on basis of right and wrong.* Use the statement to guide your thoughts and discuss the ethical dilemma in the case study.

Case study discussion 3 (A)—ethical issues and dilemma

Ethical dilemma, as noted earlier, *could arise when difficult ethical problem presents two or more possible options aimed at resolving the ethical problem. The options presented for consideration is either equally desirability or equally undesirable. The situation in itself does* not seem *to present any criteria for choosing between the options.* Thus, the ethical dilemma in the case at hand arises due to the patient refusing life-saving treatment. Mr. BB, a sixty-nine-year-old grandfather, has religious beliefs that conflict with the advice of the nurses and the wishes of his family. In other words, the main ethical dilemma in this case study arises because of the conflict of ethical principle of beneficence and respect for autonomy. For example, the nurses involved in the care of Mr. BB were not able to discharge their duty of beneficence and at the same time respect his autonomy. Respecting his right of autonomy means that the nurses could not fulfill their duty to act in his beneficence or best interests, which ultimately led to his death.

Although, Mr. BB had lost consciousness on few occasions, he was alert most of the time and aware of the risks of not taking the blood transfusion and potential for losing his life. The ethical dilemma raises complex questions such as the following:

- Should his rights of autonomy be respected in favour of beneficence?
- What effect has the accident had on his mental capacity in terms of exercising his right of autonomy?
- Has the accident affected his judgement?
- Is his mind sound to refuse giving consent?
- If he is not of sound mind, can the family or the nurses decide for him?
- Does his religious belief matter?
- Should his age and health status be deciding factors?

Finally, these complex questions must be answered in any attempt to resolve the ethical dilemma. In the following chapter 7, discussion 3(B) will attempt to resolve the ethical dilemma by demonstrating that Mr. BB made an informed decision not to take the treatment. Thus, his right of autonomy overrides any need to act in his beneficence.

Summary

This chapter attempted to consider common ethical issues, which may give rise to dilemma in nursing and social work practice. As you noted earlier, ethical issues, such as conflicting ethical principles, refusing to give consent, agreeing in the best interest of patient or client, giving information, and balancing the need of patient or client against that of others and equitable distribution of services and resources, could transform into ethical dilemmas. To reinforce this view, we used case study discussion 3(A) to illustrate how; for example, conflict between acting to benefit (beneficence) Mr. BB and respecting his autonomy (respect for autonomy) gave rise to ethical dilemma. In the following chapter, we intend to use the same case study and subsequent discussions to demonstrate that a successful resolution of ethical dilemma would depend on the decision maker's logical approach and the process used to resolve the ethical dilemma.

Chapter 7

Moral Reasoning as Basis for Resolving Ethical Dilemmas

Some scholars suggest that the development of moral reasoning abilities is crucial for handling ethical dilemma in care practice. The scholars argue that it is so given the discriminatory, paternalistic, egocentric, prejudice, self-justification, and other unethical tendencies of some care professionals. They added that the unethical tendencies of these professionals can never be totally eliminated but could be minimised or controlled through development of moral reasoning capabilities (Paul, and Elder, 2005). This view could be supported when one considers *moral reasoning as involving individual or collective thinking process that aims to establish, through rational analysis, whether a decision is right (ethical) or wrong (unethical).* In other words, the development of moral reasoning abilities could help nursing and social work professionals to know whether a decision is ethical or unethical.

One scholar suggests that when care professionals face ethical dilemmas in practice, they sometimes act impulsively or instinctively, and sometimes they pause to deliberate whether such action is right or wrong (Richardson, 2007). The later action is *moral reasoning, which involves thinking about ethical dilemmas, deliberating whether action taken to resolve it is right or wrong, and reaching a decision with the help of judgement and rational analysis.* In such deliberations, the action taken and decision reached may be justified by using ethical theories or an integrated body of rules and principles (Coughlin, 2006). There are different moral reasoning approaches but we found three that seem more appropriate in nursing and social work practice. The three approaches to moral reasoning consist of the four principles'-based approach, the value-based approach, and the legal-based approach, which are illustrated below using case study discussions 3(B-D).

Four principles' approach to moral reasoning

As noted elsewhere in this book, one area in which ethical principles have obvious practical value in nursing and social work practice is decision making. We suggest that *nurses and social workers should embrace all of the four ethical principles in decision making for several reasons, but primarily because they underpin the range of duties that they owe to those in their care, especially the duty to act ethically by making the best interest of those in their care top priority*. For example, the ethical principle of autonomy would allow nursing and social work professionals to respect the right of self-determination of those in their care; non-malficence would help them decide on how not to intentionally engage in any act that risk harming those in their care and indeed others; beneficence would allow them to decide on how best to contribute to the welfare of those in their care; and justice would help them decide on how to treat those in their care according to their individual needs. The importance of these ethical principles prompted Beauchamp and Childress (1994) to state that ethics in care concerns both professionals' duties and patients' rights and concentration on the four *prima facie* principles.

Pertinent to case study 3 are the issues of exercising right of autonomy by refusing to consent to the beneficence of a blood transfusion, which gave rise to ethical dilemma. In other words, the ethical dilemma culminate in the nurses having to make a decision where there is conflict between Mr. BB's right of autonomy and the need to discharge their duty of beneficence to him. There is no clear-cut right (ethical) or wrong (unethical) either way. We intend to use model answer 3(B) below to demonstrate how the ethical dilemma could be resolved through application of the four principles' approach to moral reasoning.

Discussion 3(B)—Ethical principles' approach to moral reasoning

The ethical principle of autonomy, as you may recall from Chapter 5, could be used when trying to justify Mr. BB right of autonomy or right to be self-governing. The nurses have obligation under the principle to develop Mr. BB's ability to be self-directing by encouraging him to make his own decisions and to act on his beliefs and values. To strengthen the point made earlier, his decision needs to be informed. This would require the nurses to ensure that information given to him is accurate, freely given, and voluntarily received in advance or before he made his decision not to take the blood transfusion. In fact, the nurses did try to convince him and provided him with all the necessary information to help him make informed decision, but he totally refused the treatment. However, we do not know whether the information given to him by the nurses includes helping him to understand how his decisions and belief may affect his family who are advocating for the blood transfusion.

If, on the other hand, he lacks capacity to make his own decisions and acts on his own belief, the nurses and the doctor caring for him in discussion with his family may decide to act in his best interest. In other words, such decision could be reached during a *best interest* meeting involving his family members, the nurses and other members of the health-care team caring for him. We know from facts in the case study that apart from few occasions when he drifted in and out of consciousness, he was alert most of the time. This means that he was likely to be autonomous when he made his informed decision. It is important to emphasize at this point that even if Mr. BB is not fully competent and so not legally competent to refuse the treatment, ethically his decision must be given consideration by the nurses caring for him to the best of their ability. We must also add that there is no requirement for an autonomous decision to be the correct decision; if so, patients' needs and values would be disrespected given the nature of paternalistic tendencies of some health-care professionals.

To strengthen the point made earlier, an autonomous decision is one that is informed: Has Mr. BB been given information about the consequences of refusing the blood transfusion in a manner that he could understood? Has he been supported to weigh values and beliefs against the consequences of having or refusing the blood transfusion? The ethical principle of autonomy opposes making a decision that could force him against his will, even when the decision is intended to produce beneficial outcome to him. However, the nurses have an obligation under the ethical principle of beneficence to ensure that his welfare becomes paramount consideration when making decision about his care. To reinforce the point made in Chapter 5, Mr. BB's *right of autonomy has overriding power over any paternalistic or beneficence act of the nurses.*

The principle of beneficence conflicts with the principle of autonomy when Mr.BB made the decision that the nurses and his family do not think will benefit him. It is imperative to consider both the long-term and short-term effects of overriding Mr. BB's decision to refuse the blood transfusion to arrive at correct decision. For example, in the short term, Mr. BB may distrust nurses and other health-care professionals and may also be reluctant to seek medical help in the future. In the long term, he would benefit from the blood transfusion by staying alive. On the other hand, if his autonomy was respected in the short term, he would be happy that his wish had been respected. In the long term, however, he would die. Thus, the nurses would have to weigh the benefit of acting according to ethical principle of beneficence against the harm he would suffer as a result of failing to respect his autonomy. As you will read in the discussion 3(D), if his autonomy is proven, his wishes cannot be overridden in the interest of beneficence.

The ethical principle of non-malficence, on the other hand, would guide decision to prevent harm to him. Mr. BB will in no doubt be harmed if he is forced against his will to take the blood. Thus, the ethical principle of non-malficence could be used to justify the decision not to engage in the blood transfusion against his will. On the other hand, the nurses could apply the ethical principle of justice to guide their decision to treat Mr. BB as an individual and according to his unique needs and belief irrespective of the apparent difference between him and others who do not share his faith. To emphasis the point made in Chapter 5, the nurses have obligation under the principle to act fairly and just to all those in their care and at the same time respect their human rights. Thus, they could use the principle to justify decision to be fair and impartial in the way they respected his religious belief.

The application of the four principle-based approaches will not be complete without consideration of the ethical theories explored in Chapter 4. As you noted in Chapter 5, ethical theories are based on the ethical principles and they provide the framework to support ethically correct decisions. The individual ethical principle lays emphasis on different aspects of an ethical dilemma and lead to the most ethically correct resolution according to the guidelines within the ethical theory itself. In other words, the individual ethical theory attempts to hold fast to the ethical principles that lead to success when trying to make correct ethical decision (Rainbow, 2002). For example, the ethical theory of deontology states that people should hold fast to their obligations and duties when analysing an ethical dilemma. This is to say that the nurses caring for Mr. BB have a duty to give him the blood transfusion that will save his life irrespective of the consequence. This is because under the ethical theory of deontology upholding one's duty is what is considered ethically correct. The *principle of beneficence guides the moral duty under the ethical theory of deontology to do what is ethically correct or justifiable.* As discussed earlier, the obligation to promote welfare of those in one's care becomes paramount consideration when applying the ethical principle of beneficence. The ethical theory of deontology is often referred to as non-consequential theory. Consequential theory as noted in Chapter 4 maintains that the moral status of an action is determined by the goodness or badness of its consequences. Utilitarianism is a type of consequentialism where one justifies a decision made regarding the best course of action by simply applying a cost-benefit analysis to the situation. The greatest happiness for the greatest number of people is most acceptable calculus for determining best course of action under ethical theory of utilitarianism. Consequentialists, would justify the best course of action by calculating the consequences or outcome of a decision, and if the benefits of the outcome are outweighed by the risks of either not performing the action or performing some other action, then the action is considered as ethically acceptable (Carter, 2002). Thus, application of the ethical theories would help the nurses decide on the outcome or consequence of their action if they decide to carry out the blood transfusion against Mr. BB's wishes, which could be measured in terms of benefit to him. For example, if his wish was to be respected, he would benefit by being happy in the short term but may suffer pain and die in the long term. Thus, the nurses would have to weigh the consequence of acting to give blood or not to give blood and to make decision that would benefit in fairest and most just means available. This means that the theories, values, ethical principle of justice, and beneficence at the same time (Ridley, 1998) have potential for resolution of the ethical dilemma.

The theory of virtue, on the other hand, involves placing importance on the character of the nurses rather than on the action they had taken. Thus, it is their morals, reputation, and motivation that would be taken into account when rating their unusual and irregular behaviour that is considered wrong (unethical). For example, if the hospital or the ward had a reputation for disrespecting the autonomy of those in care, the nurses are more likely to be judged harshly for ignoring Mr. BB's wish not to have the blood transfusion because of the consistent track record of past behaviour. This means that virtue values acting to benefit (beneficence) and respect the rights (autonomy) of those in care.

However, the four principles' approach has been particularly criticised by some scholars for being too superficial or making light of complex ethical dilemmas (Thomasma, 1993; Gert *et al*, 1997; Schenck, 2002). In defense of this criticism, supporters of the principles, such as Cribb (2007), suggests that they are not designed to offer a quick fix but rather to provide a framework for good ethical thinking and decision making. In making an ethical decision, therefore, the four principle-based approaches to moral reasoning may not necessarily provide nursing and social work professionals with answers to all ethical dilemmas they are likely to face in practice. However, *the four principle-based approaches will inform their practice and allow them to make decisions that are morally justifiable.*

As noted from this section, moral reasoning requires an in-depth understanding and application of ethical theories and principles to reach justifiable ethical decisions. The principles are useful only when manifested in one's behavior and embodied in one's decisions (Paul and Elder, 2005). Ethical theories, on the other hand, as noted earlier, attempt to follow the ethical principles in order to be applicable to ethical issues in practice. The theories could be applied in combination in order to attain the most ethically correct resolution of ethical dilemma. The combined application of the ethical theories would provide opportunity for one to use a variety of ways to analyse ethical dilemmas in order to reach the most ethically correct decision possible (Rainbow, 2002). Thus, in making an ethical decision, nursing and social work professionals need to examine the dilemma and see how each of the theories and principles may relate to issues giving rise to the dilemma. In some cases, the theories and principles may throw enough light and provide means of resolving the ethical dilemma. In other cases, the nursing and social work professionals may have to look outside the theories and principles to find a solution to the ethical problem. Values, as will be discussed in the next section, will help guide decision and, like ethical theories and principles, would provide justification for one's decision.

Value-based approach to moral reasoning

Values underpin the work of nurses and social workers in every setting and have been clearly defined and discussed in Chapter 1 of this book. The process of ethical decision-making may be influenced by values. The value-based approach to moral reasoning as used in this book involves a decision-making process that is based on an analysis of the value conflicts, which may have given rise to ethical dilemma and application of professional values aimed at resolution of the ethical dilemma.

More often than not, ethical dilemmas do have inherent value-based components (Boland, 2006). The Care Sector Consortium established a value base of care practice in 1992, which became clear guidelines on ethical issues for the first time, culminating in a set of five core values that health and social care professionals should follow. The core values required to guide decision in practice include the following:

- Promoting anti-discriminatory practice
- Maintaining confidentiality of information
- Promoting and supporting individual rights to dignity, independence, choice, and health and safety
- Acknowledging individuals' personal beliefs and identity
- Supporting individuals through effective communication (CTAD, 1998)

Since the publication of the above value base, many care organisations have developed their own core values. For example, as a registered nurse, you are personally accountable for your practice. In caring for patients and clients, you must respect the patient or client as an individual, obtain consent before you give any treatment or care, protect confidential information, co-operate with others in the team, maintain your professional knowledge and competence, be trustworthy, and act to identify and minimise risk to patients and clients. These are the shared values for all registered nurses in United Kingdom (NMC, 2004). The Department of Health view of nursing core value includes the following: patient safety, care, respect, involvement, and the need for the nurse to be there unconditionally for the patient (DOH, 2006a).

In a report reviewing evidence about the principles and values, which underpinned the provision of social care services in Britain, Waine *et al* (2005) outline the following core values, which must be pursued in the provision of services: independence, citizenship, empowerment, social inclusion, respect for diversity, care, and protection for vulnerable people, children and young people, and the community.

The National Occupational Standards for Social Workers clearly outlined the following core values that the social workers must uphold in practice: all social workers must have respect for individuals, families, carers, groups, and communities regardless of their age, ethnicity, culture, level of understanding, and need. Social workers must be able to empower individuals, families, carers, groups, and communities in decisions affecting them. They must be honest about the power invested in them, including legal powers and their roles and resources available to meet needs. He or she must respect confidentiality, and inform individuals, families, carers, groups, and communities about when information needs to be shared with others. Finally, all social workers must be able to challenge discriminatory images and practices affecting individuals, families, carers, groups, and communities and put the individuals, families, carers and groups first (NOS, 2002).

These values like ethical principles discussed earlier often conflict with one another giving rise to ethical dilemma in nursing or social work practice. For example, social work values, such as self-determination, often conflict with resource-led agency policy giving rise to ethical dilemma (Preston-Shoot et al, 2001). Conflict of values is often very problematic for nursing and social work professionals as they have to determine which value should be given priority against the other. In reference to social work, Boland (2006) posited that more often than not value conflicts entail choosing between courses of action where none of the available options or alternatives seem to provide acceptable resolution to an ethical dilemma. Yet the Central Council for Education and Training in Social Work's (CCETSW) Requirements do not clarify what competent social work professionals should do to resolve such dilemma (Preston-Shoot et al, 2001). The following discussion 3(C) aims to illustrate value conflict, culminating in ethical dilemma and how application of professional values could guide decision that would help resolve the dilemma. Professional values as noted in Chapter 1 are the guiding beliefs and principles that are reinforced by ethical codes and influence what one does in nursing or social work practice. Ethical code, on the other hand, and as noted in Chapter 3, is outlined broad range of values and principles on how nurses and social workers should behave when faced with difficult situation. The value and principles are necessary as nursing and social work professionals are held to account for their action or in action and ultimate responsibility for decisions taken during professional practice. The following section, case study discussion 3(C) would discuss example of value conflict.

Case study discussion 3(C)—Value conflict

In the case study 3, ethical dilemmas arose when the nurses caring for Mr. BB had to choose between courses of action where none of the available options or alternatives seem to provide acceptable resolution to the ethical situation (Boland, 2006). The courses of action centre on whether to respect Mr. BB as an individual with its own values and beliefs or decide to remove the risk of death if he refuses the blood transfusion. These competing obligations raise questions such as which value takes priority, respecting Mr. BB's values and beliefs or identification and minimisation of any risk of harm or death to him. The Nursing and Midwifery Council Ethical Code of Conduct (2004) provides formal direction on standards to guide the nurses' decision. The code has specific values, which were discussed earlier but included on a personal level awareness of diverse values and beliefs within modern societies. Mr. BB's belief is the reason for refusing blood transfusion and therefore imperative that the nurses must respect his wishes. As long as Mr. BB is competent, he has the right to either accept or decline treatment and to be fully involved in any decision making. The nurses, on the other hand, must respect his right to decide whether or not to undergo the health-care interventions as long as he is legally competent (NMC, 2004). In other words, the ethical dilemma which arises from the conflict of value could be resolved by respecting Mr. BB's values and beliefs.

Values do not share the same power with law, yet they are interlinked and form an integral part that must be considered when making ethical decision within nursing and social work practice. Values are meant to guide ethical decision, yet the development of values is influenced by laws. This is probably why NMC (2008) emphasises the importance of legislation and the need for nurses to demonstrate both personal and professional commitment to the laws governing their practice. In reference social work, Long and Roche (2001) stated that law is central to social work, regulating practice, ensuring accountability, and providing social work professionals with the power and authority to work effectively in practice. It is requirements of social work education that all qualifying social workers must be competent in social work law. Thus, all social work students must be supported with opportunities to develop knowledge and understanding of the legal framework for social work and must develop skills in its application in practice (GSCC, 2002; QAA, 2008).

Finally, a code of ethics as noted above provides guideline for ethical decision-making based on values that should be embraced by nursing and social work professionals involved in ethical decision-making. We would like to emphasize at this juncture that *ethical code based on values is a guideline and not a behavioural code. It does not specify the behaviour that a nurse or a social worker is obliged to utilise in decision making but rather gives the values upon which an ethical decision is based.* Thus, one is encouraged to reflect on knowledge of values gained from reading this chapter in conjunction with the laws, which govern most things one does in nursing or social work practice. We also encourage our readers to consider legal reasoning discussed below as it involves decision-making processes to resolve any conflict arising from legal rule and value standards. More so, to resolve the ethical dilemma, there is need to explore values, ethical theories, and principles, as well as legal implications of all decisions (McDermott, 2002).

Legal-based approach to moral reasoning

One area in which critical thinking has obvious practical value in nursing and social work practice is legal reasoning. Just like miscarriage of justice results when judges, jurors, or lawmakers decide badly, bad decision by nursing or social work professionals would have adverse consequence for those in their care. Thus, all nursing and social work professionals have obligation to understand at least in general terms how the law works and what distinguishes good legal reasoning from bad one. We cannot over emphasise the importance of law in nursing and social work practice. Some scholars argue that law determines what nursing and social work professionals can or cannot do through legitimate actions and empowers them to develop their capacity for making judgements and for identifying practice standards, for which they are accountable (Tingle, 2001; Braye, 2005). In other words, law governs almost all activities carried out by nurses and social workers in practice. *The decisions and actions of nursing and social work professionals are subject to certain predetermined legal duties and obligations, which are derived from various Acts of Parliament (statutory laws), common laws (case laws), and regulations (EU laws).* Thus, it is the responsibility of a nurse or social worker to understand the legal duties and obligation that are applicable in their professional practice area and how they impact on their relationship with colleagues and those in their care. More so, they are responsible for any decision they make and thus should ensure that such decision is, at least, in line with the law (GSCC, 2002; NMC, 2008). Yet Cox (2010) observed that many nurses have poor understanding of the law in relation to health-care practice and that there is no evidence to show that this educational deficit has been addressed. In response to this view, we listed below the common ethical issues and most relevant laws that nursing and social work students most learn. We suggest they familiarise themselves with their duties and obligation under the laws outlined in Table 2 as they are accountable to the public and those in their care through the laws. Furthermore, the knowledge of the laws and their application would help one make decisions when conflict arises between the laws and ethical issues and find justification for any decisions made. However, *law has over-ruling power over ethical principles and values; and as noted earlier governs all actions and decisions in nursing and social work practice.*

Table 2: Adapted from CTAD (1998)

Common Ethical Issues	Relevant laws
Agreeing in best interest	Sex Discrimination Act, 1975 Race Relations Act, 1976 Mental Health Act, 1983 The Children Act, 1989 Human Right Act, 1998 The Equality Act, 2010
Conflicting moral imperatives	Race Relations Act, 1976 Disability Discrimination Act, 1995 Human Right Act, 1998 The Equality Act, 2010
Assessing risks to individuals and groups	Mental Health Act, 1983 The Children Act, 1989 NHS and Community Care Act, 1990 Human Right Act, 1998
Refusing to give consent	The Children Act, 1989 Family Reform Act, 1969 Mental Health Act, 1983 Mental Capacity Act, 2005 Human Right Act, 1998
Giving information	Access to Personal Files Act, 1987 Access to Health Records Act, 1990 Data Protection Act, 1998 Human Right Act, 1998 Mental Capacity Act, 2005

The knowledge of these laws and their application in nursing and social work practice should be gained to facilitate application of legal reasoning approach. Some scholars argue that legal reasoning starts with the rule of law and the rule is the law. They added that legal reasoning use by jurors when they find a criminal defendant guilty or not guilty and by lawyers when they advise a client about the legal penalty of a possible course of action is a thinking process in which legal rules are used to answer legal questions (Benjamin and Templin, 2003). Legal reasoning as used in this section refers to decision-making process that is based on an analysis of any conflict of legal rule with ethical code or value that gives rise to ethical dilemma and application of relevant laws governing nursing and social work practice to justify any decision made in an attempt to resolve the dilemma.

As stated elsewhere in this book, nursing and social work professionals often confront difficult ethical dilemmas in practice. Law is a system of rules, and rules can conflict giving rise to ethical dilemma. Ethical dilemma may also arise when nursing and social work professionals make decisions that are compatible with legal rules but not consistent with ethical codes and/or values; or consistent with ethical codes and/or values but not with legal rules. They may also face ethical dilemma when they believe that actions permitted by the law would violate their professional values or when actions that would violate the law are necessary to comply with their professional values.

In R v Avon County Council ex parte M [1995] Family Law 66, it was the court, and not the local authority, that upheld the right of a young man with Down's syndrome to have his psychological needs taken into account in determining overall needs and to have his choice of accommodation respected. In R v North Yorkshire County Council ex parte Hargreaves [1997] 1 CCLR 104, the court also held that despite problems of communication, a woman with severe mental disability should have had her preferences taken into account when assessing her need for respite care. These cases cited by Preston-Shoot *et al* (2001) and many more may have led to the criticisms of professional values as an idealistic set of abstractions, which provide inadequate guidance on the dilemmas that professionals increasingly encounter.

This may have prompted some scholars to call for values requirement to be clearly spelt out and located in the legal, organisational, and political contexts within which professionals practise (Hugman and Smith,1995, cited in Preston-Shoot *et al,* 2001).

However, legal systems sometimes include rules for resolving conflicts, and sometimes they do not. Where conflict-resolving rules are lacking or have unclear application, nursing and social work professionals could successfully resolve such dilemmas by applying the legal reasoning model. The legal reasoning model we propose is IRAC (Issue, Rule, Analysis, and Conclusion). IRAC is a good model which allows professionals to analyse and resolve any legal problem (Benjamin and Templin, 2003). The IRAC legal reasoning model will be used to illustrate resolution of the ethical dilemma in the case study 3 and recommended as a supplementary decision-making model to the one proposed in Chapter 8 of this book with subtle differences. The IRAC framework is illustrated as follows:

Issue—identify the legal issue(s) in the case study or situation in question.
Rule—identify the legal rule relevant to the issue or fact
Analysis—apply the legal rule to the facts in the case or situation.
Conclusion—discuss the outcome of the analysis (Guenther, 2009).

Case study discussion 3(D)—Conflict of legal rule and ethical code and/or values

As discussed elsewhere in this book, the ethical principle of respect for autonomy has overriding power over other principles. In other words, if Mr. BB is autonomous, his right of autonomy will overrule any beneficence act towards him. The dilemma for the nurses caring for him arises when his right of autonomy which is compatible with his legal right to refuse treatment conflicts with their professional values and requirement to act in his best interest which is consistent with the ethical principle of beneficence (NMC, 2008). We will attempt to resolve the dilemma using the IRAC framework. IRAC is a pneumonic formulation, which stands for Issue, Rule, Application, Conclusion that provides a tool for analysis of legal issues and guides one towards a justifiable conclusion (Buckley and Okrent, 2004) and are applied as follows:

- The first stage is to identify the legal issue(s). The stage would allow one to discuss what the law has to say. The legal issue in the case study 3, centres on whether or not Mr. BB is competent to refuse a life-saving treatment.
- The second stage is to identify the legal rule relevant to the issue(s). It is unlawful to treat Mr. BB without his consent. Section 1 of the Mental Capacity Act (MCA) (2005) states that everyone is competent to give consent unless otherwise can be proven. To prove whether or not Mr. BB is competent to consent, Section 3 of the MCA (2005) must be applied. The rule under this section requires Mr. BB to be given all relevant information about the treatment which would help him make informed decision. On his own part, he needs to show understanding of the information given, be able to retain the information, use or weigh up the information, and clearly communicate his decision. As noted earlier, consent must be informed, given freely and voluntarily. Thus, as long as he gives informed consent and legally competent, his wish must be respected. He also has a right not to be tortured or mistreated under Article 3 of the Human Rights Act (1998). Giving him the blood transfusion against his wish is tantamount to mistreatment and a breach of his rights under the Article 3.

As stated earlier, law governs professional practice, and when a legal decision is made, one needs to justify it by stating exactly which law is being relied upon. This will in no doubt present variety of challenges for some nurses and social workers. Mr. BB, for instance, exercised his right of autonomy when he declined the life saving treatment and subsequently died; yet the nurses would have to justify their decision to let him take his own life. On the other hand, there is no legal justification for the comments made by one of the nurses, that, 'she did not see any reason for the fuss, he is old and going to die soon'. The other nurses ignored the comments and did their best to persuade Mr.BB to take the treatment. However, such comments were based on prejudice. The nurse may have to face professional misconduct hearing and subsequent disciplinary action. This is because her comment was disrespectful to the diginity of her patient and thus breached NMC (2008) professional codes of conduct.

As noted in the case study 3, the hospital policy is to respect the wishes of patients in cases where they are able to make their wishes known in accordance with the rules under the MCA (2005). Thus, he made his decision fully aware that his life was at risk and the nurses had no choice except to respect his autonomy. At this juncture, one could argue that his best interest was served by respecting his wish.

- The third stage is for the purpose of legal analysis which would allow one to search for material facts in the case that fit the elements of the legal rule. The Article 2 of Human Rights Act (1998) protects Mr. BB's right to life. He is also protected under Article 3 from torture or mistreatment. These legal rules place a duty on the nurses caring for him to prevent death or harm to him. For example, giving the treatment against his wish amounts to mistreatment or harm which is against his right under Article 3 of the Human Rights Act (HRA) 1998. He tortured himself and took his own life when he exercised his right of autonomy and refused the treatment. Thus, his death and the the pain he suffered did not amount to breach of his rights under Article 2 and Article 3 of the HRA (1998).

As there is no specific law on consent, the nurses could justify their decision by citing legal rules derived from case laws. For example, Dimond (1999) cited a similar case to the one under consideration, which involved a mother who had given birth to twins. The patient who was a Jehovah's Witness refused a blood transfusion. The court ruled that as there was no evidence to deem her incapable of making such a decision, her autonomy, beliefs, and values were to be respected. Similarly, a Daily Mail Online article reported that a 22 year old young mother died after giving birth to twins because her faith prohibited a life-saving blood transfusion. She had signed a form before giving birth refusing any form of treatment involving blood product. Staff at the hospital explained the consequence of her decision and pleaded with her and her family who were also Jehovah's Witnesses to allow the transfusion. They all refused the treatment and claimed that blood transfusions are prohibited by the Bible (Hull, et. al., 2007). In the case of Malette v Shulman (1998) 63 OR (2d) 243, following a road traffic accident, a doctor made a life-saving judgement to administer blood to an unconscious patient despite a Jehovah's Witness card requesting 'no blood transfusions under any circumstances.' The patient survived and successfully sued the doctor, who was liable in tort law for battery. These cases provide justification for the nurses' decision to respect Mr. BB's informed decision not to receive the blood transfusion when it was meant to safe his life.

On the other hand, if they had forced Mr. BB against his will to have the blood transfusion, it would amount to malpractice. A charge of negligence is often brought against professionals for malpractice. *Malpractice in law is a form of 'tort' resulting from any act of omission or commission, which violates legal or professional standard of care that proves harmful to a patient or client.* In court of law, a patient often referred to as plaintiff or claimant must prove three tests for a successful malpractice claim. The tests are duty of care, breach of duty of care, and proof of harm. For example, first, Mr. BB would have to prove that the nurses who will be referred to in court as the defendants owed him a legal duty of care. The duty of care was defined in case law (common law), especially in the landmark case, Donohue v Stevenson (1932). Lord Atkin's definition of duty of care in the case is complex and written in legal terminologies. We are happy to simplify the definition as *'one owes a duty of care to someone who will be harmed by ones action or inaction, which one ought to have in mind before committing the act.'* In other words, *a legal duty of care in 'tort law' is an obligation imposed on an individual requiring that the individual adhere to a standard of reasonable care while performing any act or omission that could foreseeable harm others.* It is evident from these definitions that the nurses owed Mr. BB a duty of care. Second, Mr. BB would have to prove that the nurses breached the duty of care owed to him. The duty of care so owed to him was breached through failure to conform to the relevant standard of care and forcefully giving him the blood transfusion. The standard of care is proved or denied by expert testimony or application of 'Bolam Test' by the court.

In examining evidence adduce by the nurses (the defendants), the court may apply "Bolam Test" to establish whether or not their action or inaction conforms to the way ordinary, reasonable, and competent professional would act under the same or similar circumstances. Third, the breach of the legal duty of care caused him harm and most importantly that the breach of duty was a 'proximate cause' of the harm suffered. Proximate cause in law is defined as an event sufficiently related to a legally recognisable harm to be held as the cause of that harm. For an act to cause harm, the two tests that must be proved in law are: proximate and cause-in-fact. Proximate (or legal) cause is a legal limitation on cause-in-fact. Cause-in-fact, on the other hand, is determined by the "but-for" test; but for the action, the result would not have happened (Rottenstein, 2011). Mr. BB could claim psychological harm from ex-communication by members of his religious sect for having the blood transfusion, nervous break down or any material loss.

These legal rules, notwithstanding, Mr. BB has the 'burden of proof', which is based on balance of probability. In other words, he has to prove all the elements by a preponderance (51 per cent) of the evidence. The presiding magistrate or judge, on the other hand, must then weigh all the adduced evidence, find the facts, and determine which party's evidence is the most credible. Successful proof of negligence will entitle Mr. BB to claim monetary compensation for any harm he suffered as a result of the forced blood transfusion. In some cases, the court will order additional punitive damages against the nurses and their employers who are vicariously liable for the tort of their employee as a punishment for malpractice.

In fact, Mr. BB's wife and children agreed that he should have the blood transfusion. Unfortunately, there is no known law that allows family to decide for a competent or incompetent patient, unless they have valid Power of Attorney or Advance Directive. As Mr. BB's family neither had Power of Attorney nor Advance Directive, the nurses could justify their decision not to respect their wishes by citing the rule under the Mental Capacity Act (2005), which only allows family members to contribute during the best interest meeting. The health-care team is not under any legal obligation to consider their decision even during the best interest meeting.

Also on fact, one of the nurses made a comment to Mr. BB's relatives that she did not see "any reason for all the fuss about his refusal to accept the blood transfusion, he was old, suffering from multiple sclerosis, and going to die soon anyway". Such comment is based on prejudice and will only amount to a breach under Disability Discrimination Act (DDA) (2005), or Equality Act (2010), if acted upon. Long-term and progressive conditions, such as multiple sclerosis, count as disability under the DDA (2005). The legal rule under the DDA and Equality Acts prevents discrimination on many grounds, including age and health status. It could also be a breach of Mr. BB's right under Article 14 of Human Rights Act (1998), which prohibits discrimination, if the prejudice was acted upon. The rule under the article guarantees the enjoyment of rights and freedoms without discrimination on any ground such as sex, race, colour, language, religion, political or other opinion, national or social origin, and association with a national minority, property, birth, or other status. Thus, it is illegal to discriminate against Mr. BB on grounds of his beliefs, age, or long-term condition. The case of discrimination may be difficult to be proved against the nurse as there is no evidence that she acted on her prejudice. However, as stated earlier, the nurse could face disciplinary action. The NMC (2008) requires all nurses to act with integrity by demonstrating among other things personal and professional commitment to equality and diversity. NMC (2008) also states that nurses must not discriminate in any way against those in their care. Thus, Mr. BB's family could make a formal complaint against the nurse or consult the Independent Mental Capacity Advocate (IMCA) if there is evidence of mistreatment on grounds of mental capacity. They may also consult Patient Advice and Liaison Services (PALS) which provides information, advice, and support to help patients, families, and their carers in relation to mistreatment by doctors or nurses.

The fourth and final stage is the conclusion that should justify the decision reached through meeting the rules of relevant laws. The summary of the case is that Mr. BB died as result of his refusal to accept a life-saving blood transfusion on religious grounds. The ethical dilemma that resulted from the conflict between his rights of autonomy and beneficence duty of the nurses was resolved by the application of legal rules. As you noted, the law imposed a duty on the nurses to respect Mr. BB's autonomy even when the decision was likely to lead to his death. The NMC (2008) requires nurses to acknowledge the right of individuals with capacity to decline treatment. Mr. BB's right was also respected in line with the rules under the Mental Capacity Act (2005) and Article 3 and 14 of Human Rights Act (1998). Thus, the nurses have both professional and legal justifications for their decision.

The implications for potential future practice suggest that if a patients' capacity is evident, their decision must be respected. Although, this is not a case of emergency but it is important to note at this juncture that if it were to be a case of emergency and Mr. BB was deemed competent, his wishes could be over ruled under the doctrine of necessity. The Doctrine of Necessity is a common law doctrine which allows judges to do justice in situations not envisaged by specific provisions of the law (Shastri and Wilson, 2001). The doctrine since its development has been used in health-care practice to justify decisions or actions in the patient's best interest. For example, it was used to justify the detention of mental health patients but failed to fulfil the requirement of legality for the deprivation of liberty under Article 5 (1) of the Human Rights Act, 1998 (ECHR, 2004).

Finally, IRAC framework has been criticised by one scholar on the grounds that it presumes that those applying it should know enough law to identify issues in any legal situation. It also considers rules, yet rules still leave decision makers with discretion and *most legal arguments are won on facts and not rules.* It asks those using it to apply the law to the facts without explanation of how to apply the law to the facts and often confidently predicts an unqualified conclusion (Simpson, 2008). These criticisms, notwithstanding a *sound decision based on legal reasoning, requires careful analysis, research, and thoughtfulness before arriving at a justifiable decision. IRAC provides a framework that help one in terms of finding facts, analysing facts, identifying the relevant areas of law, and so on.* Thus, it would serve as a useful tool for decision making in both nursing and social work practice.

Summary

Eminent scholars suggest that moral reasoning is the basis for resolution of ethical dilemma and making ethical decision (Kohlberg, 1973; Bommer et al, 1991). Thus, this chapter emphasized the importance of developing moral reasoning abilities that are crucial for handling ethical dilemmas and making ethical decisions in nursing and social work practice. The chapter has used the principle-based approaches, value-based approach, and legal-based approach to moral reasoning and used case study discussion 3(B-D) to illustrate how the approaches inform practice and allow one to make decisions that are morally and legally justifiable. This is because nursing and social work professionals' ability to make quality ethical decisions are fundamental to nursing and social work practice, without which they cannot claim a deserving professional status. However, as one scholar suggests, much as principles, values, and law guide professional decisions in practice, they do not provide them with an understanding of how and the process by which ethical decisions are examined and then made (Hill, 2004). In the next chapter, therefore, we would explore models as another form of ethical decision-making paradigms and use case studies and discussions to illustrate ethical analysis and decision making process.

Chapter 8

Models of Ethical Decision-Making

As noted earlier, nurses and social work professionals often face ethical dilemmas and making ethical decisions to resolve them is in most cases a complex and difficult process. Thus, acquiring the skills necessary for dealing with the complexities and difficulties is an important step towards becoming confident in making sound ethical decisions (Dolgoff *et al*, 2005). It is obvious that *if nursing and social work professionals do not have a methodological approach for resolving ethical dilemmas, it is most unlikely that they find success in dealing with numerous difficult and complex ethical situations they face in practice.* In the absence of a methodological approach, they may have to act on impulse which may impede appropriate and sound ethical decision. Thus, the aim of this chapter is to demonstrate that decision-making frameworks or models could be a valuable tool in helping nursing and social work professionals to work through difficult ethical dilemmas and come to a sound ethical decisions.

As noted earlier and also discussed in Chapter 7, while knowledge of values, laws and ethical codes serve to provide nursing and social work professionals with the tools for making and justifying decisions, they do not provide them with methodological approach for analysing and resolving ethical dilemmas they constantly face in practice (Hill, 2004). Equally, as pointed out elsewhere in this book, existing texts on ethics discuss dilemmas from multiple perspectives and thus leaving the reader wondering which view is most likely to produce sound ethical decision (Hartsell, 2006). To make sound ethical decision aimed at resolving ethical dilemma, nursing and social work professionals may need to figure out the right thing, how to decide what is right, potential consequences of any action taken, and whether such action is right or wrong. Some scholars, on the other hand, suggest that any attempt to resolve any ethical dilemma must start with a careful analysis of the dilemma and consideration of consequence of any decision aimed at resolving the dilemma. They recommend the sort of ethical decision-making models that are intended to elucidate the decision-making process and provide professionals with a framework for conceptualising, evaluating, and resolving ethical dilemmas (Schenck, 2002; Taboada, 2004; Wells, 2007; Lorenzetti, 2010). For example, Lorenzetti (2010) considered frameworks for making ethical decisions within the consequence, duty—and virtue-based perspectives. The consequential or utilitarian framework perspective focuses on the future effects of the possible courses of action, taking into account the people who will be directly or indirectly affected by such action. Professionals applying this framework are advised to find out what outcomes are advantageous in any given situation, and identify the best ethical behavior to help them achieve the best consequences. In other words, nursing and social work professionals need to first of all identify the various courses of action available to them. Second, they need to ask themselves who will be affected by each action and what benefits or harms will be derived from each of the action or decision identified. And third, they should choose the action or decision that will produce the greatest benefits and the least harm. The ultimate goal of this framework is to help them carry out action or decision that would provide the greatest good for the greatest number of those in their care (Manuel et al, 2010). For example, a consequence-based ethicist would aim to achieve greatest benefit and minimum harm. Equally, utilitarian ethicist would aim for greatest good for the greatest number of people at minimum cost of suffering. Thus, any nursing or social work professional applying the framework would consider various options presented by any ethical problem and take a decision based on the option that will offer greatest benefit and least suffering to those in his or her care.

The framework has some distinct advantages and disadvantages. The main advantage is that it has the very pragmatic way of considering an ethical dilemma and provides opportunity for focusing on the results of an action or decision. It would work well when considering ethical issues that involve great numbers of patients or clients, especially those that might involve trade-offs between good consequences for some and bad consequences for others. The main disadvantage is that it is not always possible to predict the consequences of an action or decision when using the framework. Thus, some actions that are expected to produce good consequences might in the end produce harmful outcome. The pragmatism embraced by the consequence framework may also be a disadvantage. This is because people may react negatively to the pragmatic approach in response to the implication that the end justifies the means. In addition, the consequence framework does not include a declaration that certain things are always wrong. The most dreadful action or decision may result in a good outcome for some people and such action or decision will be considered ethical under this consequence framework.

Unlike the consequence framework, professionals applying duty framework are expected to focus on the duties and obligations they have in a given situation. This means considering what ethical obligations they have and what things they should never do (Lorenzetti, 2010). In other words, acceptable ethical conduct under this framework could be defined as doing one's duties and doing the right thing aimed at carrying out the correct decision or action. In deciding which conduct is ethical under this framework, nursing and social work professionals must ascertain whether such conduct respect the moral rights of those in their care who may be affected by such conduct. The conduct or action will be morally wrong if it violates the rights of the individuals in their care. The more serious the violation of an individual's right, the more wrongful the conduct or action will be (Manuel et al, 2010). Further more and as noted in Chapter 4, to help nursing and social work professionals decide on which conduct or action is right or wrong, deontology, which underpins duty-based ethics, would consider an action to be ethically right when it conforms to rules or duties or wrong when it fails to conform to rule or duties. This theory implies that there are rule governing every duty or role and that one should follow the rule of one's profession when faced with ethical dilemma or ethical decision in practice. In other words, decision based on professional code of conduct would be considered a moral decision. This means that nurses and social workers should consider the NMC professional code of conduct and GSCC code of practice, respectively, when making ethical decision.

For example, any nursing or social work professionals working from a duty-based framework would resist any attempt to breach the duty of confidentiality owed to a patient or client except when such breach can be justified under one of the exception rules discussed elsewhere in this book. Duty of confidentiality is considered very important by nursing and social work professionals as one of the duties enshrined in their professional code of practice.

The advantage of the duty-based framework is that it creates a system of rules that has consistent expectations of all people. For example, required duty in any ethical situation applies to everyone facing the same situation and by so doing provide opportunity for those in care to be treated equitably and fairly in accordance with their individual needs. This mirrors the ethical principle of justice, and as discussed in Chapter 5, it is a principle that demands fairness and fair play. Another advantage of duty-base framework is that it focuses on following ethical rules or duty regardless of outcome. Thus, it allows for the possibility to act ethically even when the outcome is harmful. In other words, the framework provides ethical justification for unintended harmful action. It is expected to yield the best result when one applies it to situations where there is a sense of obligation or in ethical situations in which one need to consider why duty or obligation mandates forbid certain courses of action. On the other hand, the framework's main disadvantage includes its inability to explain how one should act if the duty-driven action will produce harmful outcome. In addition, it does not explain whether an action or decision can still be justified ethically if and when it is known that it will produce harmful outcome. Furthermore, it does not help in making distinction between conflicting duties. And in most cases, it is very rigid in applying the notion of duty to everyone despite personal situation.

Virtues, as noted in Chapter 4 of this book, are characteristic traits that enable people to be and to act in ways that develop their highest potential. Virtue enables individuals to pursue ideals they have adopted such as honesty, courage, compassion, generosity, fidelity, integrity, fairness, self-control, and prudence (Manuel *et al*, 2010). As noted earlier, virtues are characteristic traits that predispose people to act in accordance with worthy goals and the role expected of them. It includes compassion, honesty, fidelity, discernment, and integrity which constitute important components of ethical decision-making.

In ethical decision-making, virtue places less prominence on which rules professionals should follow and instead focus on helping them to build up good character traits, such as kindness and generosity, which in turn, allows the professionals to make correct decisions. Virtue ethicists also stress the need to learn how to break very bad habits of character, such as selfishness, dishonesty, disrespectfulness, or aggressive behaviour. These are what Aristotelian ethical theorists considered as vices, which create obstacles in the way of becoming a good person and arriving at good decisions (Timpe, 2008).

The advantage of the virtue framework is that it tries to identify positive or negative characteristic traits that might motivate somebody to act or decide in certain way in a given situation. It focuses on the kind of person one is and what one's decision or action say about one's character. It defines ethical behaviour expected from a virtuous person in any given situation, and how the person seeks to develop his or her character. A virtuous person, on the other hand, will decide from some kind of motivation. However, the main disadvantage or the downside of the virtue framework is that certain virtues are necessary for correct moral decisions, and correct moral decisions require correct motives. In other words, virtue concerns doing the right thing, to the right person, at the right time, to the proper extent, in the correct manner, for the right reason. Doing the right thing as well as the right sort of character a virtuous person should have, have been the most critical areas of virtue ethics and yet most relevant areas to nursing and social work practice. For example, a nursing or social work professional, who behaves in a virtuous manner by exercising patience, honesty, and being trustworthy will be considered to have a good manner or have a good character (Thompson *et al*, 2006).

Finally, Lorenzetti's (2010) ethical theory-based frameworks are not intended to provide an automatic solution to ethical problems. However, it would help one identify most of the important ethical considerations in any given situation. For example, in dealing with an ethical problem using the virtue framework, one needs to find out the sort of person one should be and what will promote the development of character within oneself and community. For consequence or utilitarian framework, one needs to consider what benefits and what harms will each decision or action produce and which alternative will lead to the best overall consequences or which course of action or decision advances the common good. And consider what ethical rights do the affected parties have and which course of action or decision best respects those rights. In addition, one needs to consider which course of action or decision treats an individual in one's care according to his or her needs, except where there is a morally justifiable reason not to do so, and does not inculcate favouritism or discrimination (Manuel *et al*, 2010).

Another example of ethical decision model is 'Algorithm', which is a seven-step model intended to help nurses to deal with complex processes of resolving ethical dilemmas and make decisions. According to Schenck (2002), algorithm is a method for analysing and working up clinical ethical problems used in the Schools of Medicine and Nursing at Georgetown University. The first step in dealing with an ethical dilemma within the algorithm model is to ascertain the medical facts of the case. The second step is to assess relevant nonmedical issues. This step often poses a challenge, in that, it attempts to come to some understanding of the state of mind of the patients, the view of their illness history, their relationships with others and their social situations, the spiritual aspects of their lives, and any other factors that will help in understanding the context in which they will have to make a decision. These steps are followed by an assessment of the goods important in the case. The most immediate concern is obviously what is good for the patients medically, but that is followed closely by an attempt to understand the patients' overall good, that is, psychological good, good in terms of family and relations, spiritual good, and good in terms of the patients' preceding life history and values. While ensuring the good of the patients is the primary goal, it is insufficient by itself, for the goods of others must also be considered; acting for the good of the patients would be inappropriate if that would mean a lack of respect for the goods of others. The third step allows relevant principles to be applied to the dilemma at hand and then examined, specifying what a given principle means in this case and balancing it against the ethical claims of each of the others. According to Schenck (2002), such exercise may not be enough in terms of helping professionals to resolve an ethical dilemma, especially if patient refuses to accept autonomy as a 'de facto trump' principle. He added that principles by themselves can become mere abstractions for dealing with complex ethical dilemmas. The fourth step in the algorithm decision-making process explores the nature of the relationship. Virtue ethics could be used to addresses the nature of the relationship, that is, the nature of the relationship between the health-care professionals and their patients. Virtues such as compassion, fidelity to trust, integrity, prudence, self-effacement, justice, fortitude, and temperance are of vital importance and may guide decision that affects the relationship. For example, prudence is the virtue that disposes one to do the right thing and work towards meeting positive ends. It could be defined as practical wisdom, discerns the rightness in any particular decision, and thus gives nursing professionals the ability to choose right decision in any given situation such as the decision to act in the best interest of those in their care, their values, aspirations, needs, and beliefs. The character of nursing professionals, therefore, depends on their ability to exercise prudence in the proper application of virtues. There is no right answer to ethical dilemma, but ethical virtue can help provide justification for ethical decision in many cases. Step six of the algorithm process allows a comparison of cases at hand with any prior similar cases, which provides better guidance over and above virtue and principle to aid decision making. Finally, step seven allows suggestions or recommendations to be made in the algorithm process (Schenck, 2002).

MacDonald's (2010) model is another step-by-step guide to making ethical decisions. The model begins at step one, which recognises the moral dimension of the decision to be made. This is the first stage in the decision-making process where one is expected to recognise the impending decision as having moral significance. Step two asks the questions: Who are the interested parties? What are their relationships? These involve careful identification of all the interested parties in the decision using one's imagination and sympathy. In addition, one is required to examine the relationship between the interested parties and ask oneself the question: Do the relationships bring special obligations or expectations? The third stage involves identification of the values involved. At this stage, one is required to think through the shared values that are at stake in making the decision such as trust, autonomy, or fairness. At step four, one is expected to weigh the benefits and the burdens of one's decision. Benefit might include such things as the production of goods (physical, emotional, financial, and social, etc.) for various parties, the satisfaction of preferences, and acting in accordance with various relevant values. Burdens, on the other hand, might include causing physical or emotional pain to various parties, imposing financial costs, and ignoring relevant values. Step five asks one to look for analogous cases by thinking of other similar decisions, identify the course of action that was taken, and establish similarity in the present case or any differences. Step six requires discussion with relevant others. If time permits, discuss one's decision with all those with a stake in the decision. Gather opinions, and ask for the reasons behind those opinions. Remember that one's ability to discuss with others may be limited by the other people's expectations of confidentiality and what they consider to be in their own best interest. Step seven requires one to establish whether or not the decision accords with legal and organisational rules. Some decisions are appropriately made based on legal considerations. Others may require serious consideration, especially if they are considered illegal. Decisions may also be affected by rules set by organisation in which one works. Whether there are bad laws, or bad rules, it is always ethically important to pay attention to them. The final stage eight requires one to assess how comfortable one is with the decision by asking oneself the following questions: Is the decision one is about to take one which is wise, informed, and virtuous? And, can one live with the decision if taken? Finally, in applying the model, MacDonald (2010) advised that the order of the steps is not crucial as it may vary from one situation to the next. However, he warns that there is no guarantee that the model will lead to good decisions but would only act as a guide.

The first example of an ethical decision-making model considered earlier is unique compared to the last two examples. The model considers framework for making ethical decisions within the consequence, duty—and virtue-based perspectives (Lorenzetti, 2010), whilst the two later ethical decision-making models encompassed within the paradigms described above have several elements in common. The models suggest a logical step-by-step process for decision making. The model we propose is inclusive of elements common to most ethical decision-making models, yet unique, in that, it is comprehensive, straight forward, and offer pragmatic approach to decision making for nurses and social workers. The model is a synthesis of the scholarly works of Forester-Miller and Davis (1996), Schenck (2002), Taboada (2004), MacDonald (2010), and many other scholars who had written on ethical decision-making models. The model will challenge professionals with an ethical dilemma to determine the nature and dimension of the dilemma, generate potential courses of action, consider the potential consequences of all options and determine a course of action, evaluate the selected course of action, and implement the course of action. The model is conceptually grounded in legal rules, ethical and professional values. The synthesis allows us to create a model that is theoretically grounded, yet simple and easy to use in practice. The section below illustrates the proposed ethical decision-making model.

SIAC ethical analysis and decision-making model

Some scholars suggested that students frequently confront ethical problems in practice placement. Some of the students, they argued, lack the necessary skills for a systematic analysis of ethical dilemmas and making decisions. Some of the scholars, on the other hand, added that many of the first-year students, who did not get a formal education in ethics, do not feel confident enough to deal with the ethical problems in general (Taboada, 2004; Cohen et al, 2006). The above ethical decision-making frameworks are mostly aimed at practicing professionals and not for students. This spurred on the need to develop an effective but simple ethical analysis and decision-making model for students in practice placements and also newly qualified professional trying to get to grips with analysis of ethical problems and decision-making in practice. Thus, we developed SIAC model for use by both students and newly qualified professionals.

What is SIAC model?

SIAC is an acronym that acts as a cue for users of the model with each letter representing an aspect for analysis. For example,

S-Summarise the facts in a scenario; I-Identify and examine any ethical issues from different perspectives, that is, values, legal, and ethical; A-Apply relevant values, legal and ethical principles to the ethical issue; C-Consider all options and potential consequence of each option, decide and implement the option with least consequence. The diagrammatical representation of SIAC model is as follows:

Diagrammatical representation of SIAC model

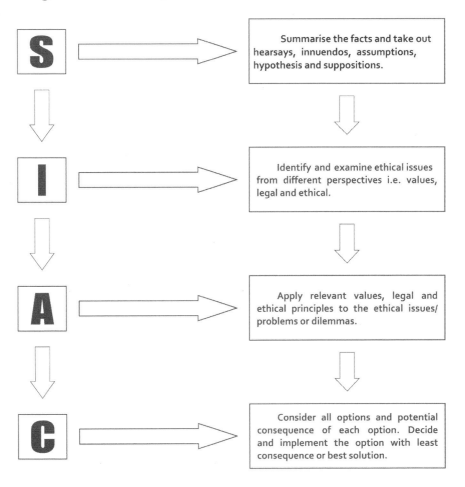

Step 1

Summary Of Issues

The first stage would allow one to summarise facts in the scenario. To achieve this, one needs to ask oneself the following questions:

- Are the issues related to one, and if so, what is it that one has done or failed to do?
- Is it related to a patient(s)/client(s), colleague(s), or significant others, and if so, what have they done or failed to do?
- Is it related to the institution, agency, or their policies and procedures? If so, what is/are the issue(s)? Can one learn more about the situation(s)?Does one know enough to make a decision?

Summarise or outline the facts, identified and remove hearsays, innuendos, assumptions, hypothesis and suppositions.

step 2

Identify relevant values, legal, and ethical issues

This second stage requires one to ask the following questions:

- Are the issues relevant to any value, legal or ethical principle?
- Is it a combination of more than one of these?
- If so, outline each principle separately and according to individual perspective (i.e. values, legal and ethical principles) and state them clearly.

step 3

Apply the identified principles to the facts identified in step 1

If one identifies any professional issues, refer to one's professional code of conducts (i.e. NMC or GSCC etc) to see how the issue should be addressed. To be able to apply one's professional code of ethics, one should read it carefully and understand its implications in relation to the ethical problem. One should do the same for any ethical and/or legal principles identified. In addition, one should decide which principles apply to the specific issue in the scenario and what to do whenever there is conflict of principles. For example, when making ethical decision, one needs to determine which principle takes priority over the others in the scenario. Ethical values are morally superior to non-ethical ones. Thus, when faced with a clear choice between such values, one should always choose ethical values over non-ethical ones. One should breach ethical value only when it is clearly necessary to advance the best interest of one's patient or client. As noted elsewhere in the chapters of this book, ethical dilemma often occurs when there is a conflict between two or more values or ethical principles. Thus, prioritising one value or ethical principle against another can help resolve ethical dilemmas. As noted earlier, also, the principle of autonomy overrides beneficicence wherever there is a conflict and the patient or client is autonomous. In other words, the wishes of autonomous patients or clients will always override the need to act in the patients' or clients' best interest.

step 4

Consider all options and implement the option that would best resolve the ethical issue, problem or dilemma

At this final stage, one should consider all available options and assess potential consequences of each option and determine the best option to resolve the ethical dilemma. Evaluate the options by asking, for example, the following questions:

- Which option will produce the most good and do the least harm? (This demands for utilitarian, beneficence and non-malficence approaches to decision making).
- Which option focus on the duties and obligations one has in a given situation? (This demands for duty-based decision-making approach).
- Which option treats people equally or fairly? (This demands for justice approach to decision making).

- Which option leads one to act as a person of good character? (This demands virtue approach to decision making).

To consider the best option that will resolve the ethical dilemma, one needs to evaluate the implications of each option in relation to patient or client, and those who will be affected by the decision and for oneself as a nurse or social worker. In addition, eliminate any options that clearly do not match the expected outcome or give rise to additional ethical problem.

One should then make a decision by carrying out a review of the remaining options and decide or implement the option or combination of options one considers best in order to resolve the ethical dilemma. Act by implementing the decision with the greatest care and attention to the concerns of all stakeholders. Reflect on the outcome by considering how one decision turns out and what one has learned from the whole process of resolving the ethical dilemma.

Finally, much as one should follow in the four different steps recommended by the SIAC model, one does not have to apply the steps in a rigid manner. The steps should rather serve as a guide to ethical enquiries, gathering of different types of information, and used in an effort to resolve an ethical dilemma. The following case studies and subsequent discussions illustrate application of the SIAC model.

Case study 4

Ms DB is an eighty-four-year-old woman and was transferred from a nursing home to the hospital with advanced senile dementia, severe heart problems, and a Do-Not-Resuscitate (DNR) order. She was bedridden and was admitted into hospital with a hip fracture, which required surgery. There was a general agreement that surgery was necessary; however, there was disagreement regarding status of her DNR order. The DNR order was apparently signed by a family member, whom all attempts to contact for clarification failed.

Exercise: Analyse Ms DB's case and discuss the main factors to be considered in any attempt at resolving the ethical dilemma using the SIAC model as guidance.

Case study discussion 4

Ms DB is an eighty-four-year-old woman with advanced senile dementia, severe heart problems, and had on her file a Do-Not-Resuscitate (DNR) order apparently signed by a family member. It was unclear what Ms DB would have preferred to do had she been able to speak for herself. This raised ethical dilemma for health-care professionals caring for her as to what should become of the DNR order should surgery be performed.

The main issues in this case study concerns status of the DNR with professional, ethical and legal implications. Some scholars suggested that medical literature contains some ambiguities on the extent of a DNR order and the resuscitative interventions it prevents during surgery and anesthesia (Fallat and Deshpande, 2004). In 2000, Department of Health (DOH, 2000) issued a circular to all NHS trusts and asked all chief executives to ensure that appropriate resuscitation policies, which respect patients' rights, were in place. In the same year, The British Medical Association (BMA,2000) published a code of practice, which stated that competent informed adults have an established legal right to refuse medical procedures in advance and that, where valid and applicable, an advance directive must be followed. The Resuscitation Council UK (2001) on their part issued the following guidelines on when to initiate DNR order:

- the patient's known or ascertainable wishes;
- the likelihood of successfully restarting the patient's heart and breathing and the patient's Human Rights, including the right to life (Article 2) and the right to be free from degrading treatment (Article 3).

According to Resuscitation Council (UK), (RCUK, 2001), a DNR order indicates that Cardiopulmonary Resuscitation (CPR) will not be initiated at the time of a patient's cardiac or respiratory arrest. This does not, however, exclude all other medical interventions. The right of Ms DB to make personal end of life decision, using DNR order must be respected by health-care professionals. As noted earlier, hospitals must have appropriate resuscitation policies, which respect patients' rights (DOH, 2000). The health care professionals, on the other hand, must respect the legal right of competent informed adults to refuse medical procedures using DNR order or any other form of advance directives. This means that Ms DB may exercise her legal right to refuse treatment or resuscitative measures using DNR order. She could also exercise her right using Advance Directives. Advance Directives has been discussed else where in this book, however, McDermott (2002), citing Diggory and Judd (2000), stated that 'advance directive' gives patients the legal right to give, or withhold, consent to specific medical treatments prospectively. The use of Advance directive should ensure that health-care professionals are aware of individual patients' wishes if their condition should deteriorate and when they suffer loss of mental capacity.

The issue of Ms DB's mental capacity is addressed in the Mental Capacity Act (2005), which may prove that she lacks capacity subject to confirmation by a qualified clinician. As noted in the case study, the DNR order was signed by a member of Ms DB's family, culminating in ethical dilemma for the health-care professionals caring for her. It is not clear what she would have preferred had she been able to speak for herself. It also raises the ethical question: Whether DNR status should continue to be maintained during surgery? It is customary with health-care professionals to apply the guiding principles of ethics to aid their decision making when resuscitation status is being considered. As noted earlier, the guiding ethical principles are non-malficence, beneficence, and respect for autonomy and justice (McDermott, 2002).

Several ethical principles guide the decision-making process of the DNR. However, we shall discuss here only the most relevant principles to Ms DB's case. The three most relevant to this scenario are beneficence, non-malficence, and respect for autonomy. To gain insight into the maintenance of the DNR during surgery, one needs to examine these ethical principles. As noted earlier, ethical principles of beneficence and non-malficence dictate that a 'people should do unto others as would want done to them'. In other words, preventing harm to others. The ethical principle of autonomy, however, may override beneficence when a decision is required to provide or withdraw life-supporting treatment (McDermott, 2002).

The ethical principles of respect for autonomy, as noted in Chapter 5, is the ability of individuals to exercise self-determination, plan their own life, and make their own decisions without any mitigation from others (Gibbons, 2008). To be autonomous, Ms DB should have the right to hold her own views, make choices, and take actions based on her personal values and beliefs (Beauchamp and Childress, 2003). Thus, it could be seen as depriving Ms DB's autonomy if the DNR order found in her file was signed by her relative without prior discussion or consent. Also, the decision taken on her behalf denies her of her basic human right to life. The right to life is clearly stated in the Human Rights Act (1998). For example, Article 2 of the Act imposes a duty to provide adequate and appropriate medical provision to preserve life. Any decision to implement the DNR order will infringe the right of Ms DB to life under the article and the health-care professionals caring for her need to be able to justify such decisions. On the other hand, the duty to preserve her life is limited by the principle of reasonableness. As McDermott (2002), citing Maclean (2000), emphasised, the right to life is protected only as far as is 'reasonable' within the concept of futility, considered by the European Court of Human Rights ruling. As McDermott (2002) citing Luce (1997), asserted that the concept of *futility* means that a patient cannot benefit from a particular medical treatment. *Futility relates to decisions that are made within a qualified clinician's expertise based on scientific evidence.*

The ethical principle of beneficence, as noted in Chapter 5, meant that health-care professionals must do good for Ms DB whilst she is in their care. The principle focuses on the positive ethical obligations owed by health and social work professionals to those in their care (Herring, 2008). Beneficence supports the use of DNR order when it is likely to be most effective. Arguably, the health-care professionals caring for Ms DB will be acting in her best interest by not carrying out CPR when it will help prevent further suffering and find justification in the ethical principle of beneficence. The ethical principle of non-malficence, on the other hand, argues against performing CPR when the outcomes are harmful or when usage is inappropriate for Ms DB's condition. Primum non nocere, meaning, above all do not harm, is a well-established statement for all health and social work professionals (Herring, 2008). The principle requires that harm should not intentionally be done to those in care and indeed any other person. Thus, under the principle, health-care professionals caring for Ms DB have obligation not to inflict harm on her (Beauchamp and Childress, 2003).

The most relevant professional issue in this case study is achieving the best interest of Ms DB. Medical professionals have traditionally focused on quantity of life and not quality. Thus, to allow Ms DB to die as required by DNR order would be seen as regrettable by most health-care professionals. In addition, *a paternalistic approach to health care, as noted earlier, demands that beneficence should rightly take precedence over respect for autonomy because professionals have superior knowledge to determine what is in the best interests of patient.* However, paternalistic decision-making is considered inappropriate as it does not consider ethical and legal rights of patients (McDermott, 2002).

The primary goal of health and social work professionals is to maximise benefit and minimise harm to those in their care. In health-care, as noted earlier, emphasis is usually placed on quantity of life and not quality. It is not surprising, therefore, to note that in practice medical paternalism allows beneficence to take precedence over respect for autonomy. However, as noted in Chapter 5, respecting the autonomy of those in care, as long as they are legally autonomous and not in an emergency situation, should legitimately take precedence over any other principle aimed at their benefit. Thus, paternalistic decision-making is inappropriate as Ms DB has legal rights, which must be considered by the health-care professionals caring for her (McDermott, 2002) citing Beauchamp and Childress (1989). This is one of the justifications for medical code of ethics which guide what doctors do in practice. For example, the General Medical Council's guidance regarding withholding or withdrawing life-prolonging treatment states that in situations where a patient has the capacity to decide, the doctor must discuss conclusions regarding any diagnosis, prognosis, and which options may be in the patient's best interest (GMC, 2006). In general, the decision not to resuscitate should be taken after due consideration of the following:

- The mentally competent patient has refused to be resuscitated.
- A valid living will (Advanced Directive) has been made by the patient as per the requirements set out in the Mental Capacity Act (2005).

- Effective cardiopulmonary resuscitation (CPR) is unlikely to be successful.
- Where successful, CPR would not be in the best interest of the patient to sustain (Dimond, 2008).

These steps must be considered in addition to any other wishes expressed by Ms DB. However, the health-care professionals caring for Ms DB have a duty to confirm the authenticity of the DNR order or find other ways of ascertaining her wishes. The DNR order indicates that Ms DB should not obtain *CPR* or other life-saving measures in the event of cardiac arrest or other medical emergencies (Smith, 2011). The authenticity of the DNR order is crucial as the health-care professionals may face court action or disciplinary action from their respective professional bodies if they fail to follow the specific guidance when executing the DNR order. Health-care professionals are accountable to the four pillars namely Professional, Ethical, Legal, and Employment accountability (Tremayne, 2008). Thus, the health-care professionals caring for Ms DB may be seen to have failed in their duty of care if they execute the DNR order signed by her family member. As the law currently stands, Ms DB's family members have no locus standi (legal authority) to make decisions on her behalf even when she is unable to make decisions for herself. However, their opinion could be sought pertaining to best interest when her quality of life issues are being considered and she is unable to express her views (McDermott, 2002). Having said that, the health-care professionals caring for her have legal obligation to have a final say in terms of what is in her best interest if she is unable make informed decisions (MCA, 2005, S.4).

If on the other hand, Ms DB signed the DNR order when she was of sane mind, the health-care professionals are obliged to respect her right not to be resuscitated. However, upholding DNR orders during surgical procedures creates ethical and legal conflicts for all surgical team members. For example, Ms DB may need general anesthesia, which involves deliberately depressing or manipulating vital signs and may lead to cardiac arrest. The best option if Ms DB's *DNR order is considered valid is to suspend the order and by so doing provide the anesthesia health-care professional the right to use all of his or her skills during resuscitative measures without having to determine if Ms DB's wishes are being jeopardised or compromised.* If she is competent and decides not to have the DNR order suspended during surgery, the health-care professionals would have no choice but honour such desire. If the health-care professionals disagree with Ms DB's wish, they should be reassigned or face risk of disciplinary action by their professional bodies or legal action from Ms DB or her family if they go against her wishes (Eckberg, 1998).

In summary, autonomy and *futility* are important considerations in Ms DB's case For example, respecting Ms DB's autonomy means that she has the right to decide how any treatment will affect her life. She makes her own decisions by the right of autonomy. If not, the health-care professionals decide solely on their own what is in her best interests, which, as we noted earlier, is paternalistic behaviour, that is, when the health-care professionals become the ultimate decision maker, imposing their own ethical and moral standards on her and against her free will. With advanced senile dementia, Ms DB's wishes are unlikely to be known. It has been argued that if patient's wishes are not known and never will be, the decision made must be in the best interest of the patient (MCA, 2005, S.4). The principle of *futility* on the other hand, based on scientific evidence, would allow a qualified clinician to decide withdrawing further treatment if Ms DB cannot benefit from it. The term *futile* has many definitions but used in this book to refer to a situation where scientific investigation confirms that intended treatment would not benefit the patient and thus requiring the patient and his or her surrogate to decide on DNR orders with informed consent. A valid DNR order means that in the event of Ms DB suffering cardiopulmonary arrest (CPA), the health-care professionals should not attempt to restore respiratory or cardiac function. The order is usually written by or for patient for whom cardiopulmonary resuscitation would be *futile*. As surgery is considered necessary and all attempts to contact Ms DB's family member who signed the DNR order has failed, the health-care team should decide to follow the hospital procedure on DNR order. Since 2000, many NHS Hospitals Trusts have appropriate resuscitation policy (DOH, 2000), which may include suspension of DNR orders when a patient undergoes a surgical procedure. Some hospitals, especially in the United States, automatically suspend DNR orders for patients undergoing surgery, whereas others provide patients the option of limited or full resuscitation *(Guarisco,* 2004). The justification for suspending DNR order during surgery has been explained earlier. However, the general advice with DNR orders regarding surgical candidates is always to clarify with competent patient. This is in addition to complying with hospital policies as well as professional values and the law pertaining to DNR orders (DOH, 2000; RCUK, 2000). In other words, any decision should be guided by the legal, ethical, and professional implications of the case. Clearly, the health-care professionals should follow the NHS trust policies and Department of Health guidelines with regards to Ms DB's rights, and the doctors involved in the case should be guided by The British Medical Association code of practice. All the health-care professionals involved in Ms DB's care must respect the Mental Capacity Act (2005), which provided that she is competent to consent or refuse treatment unless proved otherwise by a qualified clinician. They must also consider her right to life under Article 2. Ethical principles of beneficence and non-malficence allow only good to be done to her and harm prevented. In addition, if she is competent as required under the MCA (2005), her autonomy also needs to be considered as it may override beneficence when a decision is required to carry out the surgery. On the other hand, if she is incompetent, her best interest would be a good justification for carrying out the surgery. Ms DB's family members have no legal authority to make decisions on her behalf even if she is unable to make decisions or demand treatment herself (RCUK, 2001). As noted earlier, the law will only allow health-care professionals caring for her to act in her best interest if and when she is unable to make an informed decision (MCA, 2005). However, her family members can contribute to the decision-making process only when her quality of life issues are being considered (McDermott, 2002).

Finally, with the guidance provided by the SIAC model, we have been able to analyse the case of Ms DB and discuss the main factors to be considered in any attempt at resolving the ethical dilemma which arises from her DNR status, autonomy and beneficence. The following case study intends to demonstrate that SIAC model is not exclusively designed to be used by nurses; it could also be used by social workers.

Case study 5 (social work specific)

As this case study is based on an episode of care involving real people, names have been changed for reasons of confidentiality and in line with the Data Protection Act (1998), which requires protection of personal data.

Mrs. Ahmed, a fifty-two-year-old Muslim, is a hospice patient in south-east of London and in the final stage of her cancer. She is a single mother with three children: Abudu who is sixteen years old, Bintu who is thirteen years old, and Amina who is ten years old. Mrs. Ahmed's condition (cancer) has become worse in recent times. She is very weak and needs support with all activities of daily living. She is on prescription only, drug (morphine), to control her pains but complains that the drug gives her headaches and makes her feel dizzy. Mrs. Ahmed's condition has become worse in the last few days and her life expectancy is immediate to possibly fourteen days.

Mrs. Ahmed lives in a council property with her children and was working in a local factory before she was diagnosed with lung cancer. She now owes hundreds of pounds in rent arrears and is concerned about her young children. Abudu does not come home from college until late at night. Bintu is doing most of the housework and often behind in her schoolwork. Amina is missing from school because of anxiety over her mother's ill health. Despite her deteriorating condition, she is of sound mind and very articulate. She now wants to stop taking her drug because of the headache and dizziness she feels. She also wants to return home against her doctor's advice and see what she could do to stabilise her family before dying with dignity.

Exercise: Apply the SIAC model and discuss the role a social worker should play within professional, ethical, and legal boundaries to help Mrs. Ahmed feel at ease before her death and secure the future of her children.

Case study discussion 5

Mrs. Ahmed, a fifty-two-year-old woman refuses her treatment because of its side effects. She is concerned about her growing debt and her young children left to fend for themselves at home. She wants to return home and see what she could do to stabilise her family before dying. The doctor predicts that she has only two weeks to live.

Mrs. Ahmed's situation raises professional, legal, and ethical issues involving an adult client who is in hospice and in the final stage of her illness. The fact that Mrs. Ahmed is refusing to take drugs that have proven highly effective in controlling pain, raises *legal question about her competence*. As we noted in Chapter 5, the duty to respect a patient's autonomous decision presupposes that such decision is made freely by a competent person. This means that there is need to ascertain Mrs. Ahmed's competence. Section 3 of The Mental Capacity Act (2005) provides a working guide for professionals to use in order to establish a patients' or clients' competence. A person who is unable to make a decision for the purposes of Section 3 of MCA (2005) had been discussed elsewhere in this book. The concerns about Mrs. Ahmed's mounting rent arrears and worries about the children may have prevented her from making truly free decisions. It calls for further examination to establish whether her decision should be respected under such circumstances. In reaching a decision, a social worker would have to consider both the duty to benefit Mrs. Ahmed and the duty to respect her autonomy. There are two opposing considerations that may influence such decision: whether to disregard the wishes on the grounds of complaints about the drug side effects or worries about her rent arrears and her young children left to fend for themselves. In other words, the emotional state of mind may compromise autonomy, which makes her unable to make the right decisions. To declare her incompetent or unable to exercise her autonomy on the grounds of worries would be unjust. It would be fair on her and good practice on the part of the social worker to offer some counseling or psychological assistance in order to identify any unspoken reasons for refusing a beneficial treatment. It would amount to neglecting their duty to act in the best interest of Mrs. Ahmed if those caring for her should simply accept her decision without identifying and dealing with the unspoken reasons.

As noted earlier, the ethical principles of beneficence and non-malficence require nursing and social work professionals to weigh the potential risks of harm by any medical or care intervention against the probable benefits of the intervention. The principles place moral obligation on the social worker and those involved in the care of Mrs. Ahmed to act for her benefit, helping to further her important and legitimate interests and prevent any possible harm to her (Beauchamp, 2008). However, the principle of the double effect may explain why the doctor in Mrs. Ahmed's case may be justifiable in his action to prescribe drug that may produce such side effect. This principle sets the ethical criteria for the legitimacy of decisions that have well-known, unavoidable bad side effects (Taboada, 2004). In other words, the principle of double effect could be used to justify the use of drug to control pain even though it may hasten death or cause unintended side effects. The social worker may need to know that there are many cases in which the health-care professionals cannot act to benefit clients without also causing undesired harm; as long as they act within clearly defined guidelines. For example, the principle of double effect ethically legitimates such action under the following conditions:

- The act performed is not itself morally evil.
- The good effect must not be achieved by way of the evil effect.
- Only the good effects are directly intended; the bad effects are not intended but only tolerated, unavoidable or incidental.
- There is a due proportion between good and bad effects (Taboada, 2004).

It may be argued in the case of Mrs. Ahmed that the doctor prescribes morphine to control her pains knowing that the drug may cause some negative side effect. The good effect of controlling the pain was the intention while the side effects of the drug were only incidental or unintended and thus, justified the treatment.

The social worker clearly has a role to play as Mrs. Ahmed's advocate. The social workers' role in end of life care is often very difficult when it involves family issues and their approach usually starts with assessment of the complex issues and breaking them down into small manageable tasks. Starting off with simple practical problems first and work through to the most complex and by so doing gain the family's confidence in the whole process (Malcolm, 2007).

Finally, the social worker handling Mrs. Ahmed's case should make decision on how to execute the four family issues in addition to empowering her to stand up for her right whenever her autonomy is breached. The first family issue relates to sorting out her rent arrears. The second issue is to safeguard the interest of the children. The third issue is to explore the chance of reconciling Mr. and Mrs. Ahmed and encourage Mr. Ahmed to take full responsibility for care of the children after the death of Mrs. Ahmed. The fourth and finally issueis to arrange for a qualified councilor from social services to mentally prepare the children to cope with the impending death of their mother. The following section will discuss the social worker's role in dealing with these issues.

social worker's role

The key purpose of social work according to the International Association of Schools of Social work and the International Federation of Social Workers cited in NOS (2002, p. 12) is to "promotes social change, problem solving in human relationships and the empowerment and liberation of people to enhance well-being". Social workers' role include helping people to maintain independence while also promoting social justice and freedom(Malcolm, 2007).The role of the social worker was critical in resolving the professional, legal, and ethical issues raised by Mrs. Ahmed's case. For example, the question arises whether it is legitimate for her to refuse the medication because of the side effects when there are obvious benefits in terms of relieving her pains. This also raises a further question whether she was fully competent to refuse the drugs. The legal and ethical principles involved are primarily beneficence, respect for her autonomy and her mental capacity. The role of social worker in this particular scenario is different from the role of health-care professionals, in that, it will focus on providing personal help for Mrs. Ahmed and her family in solving social problems and accessing social justice. Thus, using the SIAC model, we aim to demonstrate how these various aspects of social work are fused together and used to resolve the professional, legal, and ethical issues raised by Mrs. Ahmed's situation.

A social worker has a duty to empower clients, represent their views on matters affecting them (NOS, 2002). Thus, if the social worker was aware of any facts that would suggest that the action of the doctor was not in Mrs. Ahmed's best interest, he or she has a duty to take up the matter with the doctor concerned. In other words, if the social worker was aware of the fact that Mrs. Ahmed's autonomy has been breached, she has moral and professional obligation to empower her to stand up for her right or represent her view. At the same time, the social worker in this case cannot surpass limits of her role and must work effectively as a member of a multidisciplinary team. Thus, if the doctor deemed the drug as necessary and in the best interest of Mrs. Ahmed, the social work would have to assist the doctor in order to deliver best care for Mrs. Ahmed.

The social worker also has an important role to play in sorting out Mrs. Ahmed's rent arrears and safeguarding the interest of her children. For example, the social worker could deal with the rent arrears by contacting a welfare benefit adviser. Mrs. Ahmed is likely to be entitled to disability benefits. The Disability Discrimination Act (DDA) (1995) defines a disabled person as someone who has a physical or mental impairment that has a substantial and long-term adverse effect on his or her ability to carry out normal day-to-day activities. The Disability Discrimination Act (2005) amended the definition of disability to include people with cancer and other long-term conditions deemed to be covered by the DDA effectively from the point of diagnosis, rather than from the point when the condition has some adverse effects on their ability to carry out normal day-to-day activities. In addition, as Mrs. Ahmed is under sixty-five years of age, she may be entitled to Disability Living Allowance, which is not means tested. Disability Living Allowance is for people who have mobility problems or need help with personal care such as getting up, dressed, cooking, bathing, and laundry (CLA, 2008). She may also be entitled to housing benefits. According to Shelter (2010), one may be able to claim housing benefit if one has a low income, or receiving welfare benefits. A discretionary housing payment can be paid to her if the council believes that she needs further help with housing costs. As she is ill and cannot work, she may qualify for statutory sick pay and possibly contractual sick pay from her employer for the first twenty-eight weeks of her illness. The welfare benefit adviser will calculate her entitlements, which may wipe out the debts and relieve her anxiety. The social worker could also talk to local authority about the future care of the children who are sixteen, thirteen, and ten years of age. The local authority has an obligation under the Children Act (1989) to organise a suitable care package for them. The Act imposes a general duty on local authorities to provide a range of services to 'children in need' in their area if those services will help keep a child safe and well. The social worker should ensure that the local authority decision as to where the children should live will be influenced by Mrs. Ahmed's wishes as parent, her children's wishes, and the need to place the children near their home so that they could keep in touch with friends and relatives, if this will be good for them and whether or not the brothers and sisters should be kept together (CAB, 2010). In the short term, the social services may provide home help and ease the pressure on Bintu, who is currently saddled with housework at the expense of her schoolwork. The social worker also has an important role in liaising with school and ensures that Amina does not stay away from school. Mrs. Ahmed should be encouraged to spend as much time as possible with her. The social worker could find out whether there is a window of opportunity to reconcile Mrs. and Mr. Ahmed or whether Mr. Ahmed will be willing to take full parental responsibility for the children after Mrs. Ahmed's death. There is no need to involve the children in any negotiation at this stage, especially when they have had no contact with their father for a long time. The social worker may have to initiate the negotiation by approaching Mr. Ahmed to arrange a meeting in a neutral place and help Mrs. Ahmed prepare what to say at the meeting. The first meeting is always difficult, but the social worker should rely on her problem solving skills and empowering the parties for a successful first meeting (Malcolm, 2007). The children could be involved at a later stage of the negotiation and reconciliation. The social worker should encourage all parties to talk freely with a view to reaching agreement on future care responsibilities as an alternative to local authority child care initiative.

The social worker should talk to qualified councilors from social services about preparing the children to receive the impending news of their mother's death. As children, they are inexperienced with regards to death and dying. Currently, the children do not know that their mother has about fourteen days to live. Mrs. Ahmed thought that it is in best interest of the children not to tell them. She might consider such news too distressful for the children. Her reason is understandable but inappropriate as it may not help the children to prepare for her death (Malcolm, 2007). The social worker should brief the councilor and discuss the traumatic impact of an impending sudden news of their mother's death may have on them.

SIAC model has helped us to analyse the above case study and discuss the role of a social worker in the context of end of life care. The important lesson learned from Mrs. Ahmed's case is that the health-care professionals caring for her want her to maintain good quality of life for the remaining days of her life. This is in her utmost best interest as she needs to focus her remaining time and energy on many issues that had to be sorted out. Unfortunately, she is refusing the drugs that were meant to improve her quality of life. To resolve this dilemma, the social worker should decide on how to work with her to ensure she has all the necessary information that would enable her make an informed decision as we presume that she is autonomous, unless otherwise is proven under MCA (2005). The social worker should also decide on how to work alongside Mrs. Ahmed to resolve as many as possible the family problems so that she would not die leaving a disorganised family situation behind. Experts in end of life care believe that if one dies leaving such complicated and disorganised family situations behind, it would be difficult to maintain the family in future and that subsequent fragmentation may result in social and bereavement problems at a later stage (Malcolm, 2007). Mrs. Ahmed believes that the news of her impending death would be too stressful and decides not to let the children know. The social worker should consider involving a councilor from social services who should persuade Mrs. Ahmed and make her understand the importance of mentally preparing the children for the bereavement and, in addition, encourage her to talk to her children about the impending death. The social worker should also decide on how to help her rehearse how to break the news and deal with subsequent emotions. Hopefully, such support would give Mrs. Ahmed and her children the confidence to deal with such a sorrowful situation.

Finally, we hope that the knowledge of frameworks and models gained in this chapter will help nursing and social work students deal with ethical dilemmas whilst in practice. As some scholars suggested, frameworks and models serve as useful aids in understanding and defining the critical issues, identification of individuals that may be affected by an impending ethical decision, application of relevant guidelines and courses of action that may lead to successful resolution of ethical dilemma (Loewenberg and Dolgoff, 1996; Mattison, 2000; Edward, 2009). We have used case studies discussions to elucidate these claims and demonstrate good practice in ethical decision-making. In addition, *we have considered values and ethical codes as they provide guidance for decision making in practice; ethical principles as underping most things done in practice and laws as governing nursing and social work practice.*

Summary

A reflection on the knowledge of this chapter would show that every ethical dilemma discussed is unique and has to be handled in accordance with its own merit. Having a framework or model for ethical decision-making is extremely necessary. When one practises regularly with the framework or model, it will become very familiar to one, so much so that one would work through it automatically without following the specific steps. However, successful ethical decision-making cannot depend on models and framework alone. Many of the ethical decisions one will have to make in practice will be influenced by personal judgement based on one's knowledge of values, ethical and legal obligations. Sometimes one will make ethical decision after receiving advice from professional representatives. For example, the British Association of Social Workers and Royal College of Nursing have been giving professional advice to members who request help with handling ethical dilemmas. Sometimes, one would make decisions after consultation with professional colleagues, patients or clients, and their families and friends. Other times, one would consult with one's organisational policies and procedures before making ethical decision. In health and social care organisations, such policies and procedures include the Patients' Charter found in the NHS Hospital and Community Care Charter found in the community. These charters provide guidelines on how one should decide in the best interests of those in one's care, assessing risks, giving information, maintaining confidentiality, and respecting their individual values and beliefs. They also provide information on patients' or clients' rights within service(s). Many health and social care organisations have policies written down for their employees to follow whenever they are confronted with ethical dilemmas. Some organisations provide training as part of induction for new staff. Some of the training involves exploration of ethical issues and setting up of ground rules on how to handle any ethical dilemmas the new employees may face in the course of their work. Others may include sharing and explanation of ethical policies and procedures. Most health and social care organisations provide training for all staff as part of their Continuous Professional Development (CPD) programme. In most of the organisations, such training is mandatory whilst it is voluntary in others. Either way, it is advisable to make oneself available for such training. Most often the training would help one develop skills and understanding necessary for handling ethical dilemmas in practice (CTAD, 1998).

Conclusion

This book has been about ethics and ethical decision making. Ethics permeates most things nursing and social work professionals do in practice. The professionals in most cases engage in ethical decision-making to find solutions to multitudes of ethical dilemmas in practice. The book supports the view that ethics provide the tools for sound ethical decisions (Bowles *et al*, 2006) but argues that *sound ethical decisions to a large extent would depend on one's knowledge of ethics*. Thus, a plethora of concepts, legislation, models, values, theories and principles were considered in this book to help readers gain ethical knowledge. For example, Nursing and social work professionals have to deal with complex and difficult ethical issues and conflicts giving rise to dilemmas. In response to this view, the chapter 1 of this book provided readers with key concepts that inform practice. We argued that, *ethics, morals, and value are not only theoretical concepts, but also have profound impact on the working life of nursing and social work professionals*.

In addition, since ethics permeates most things done in nursing and social work practice, chapter 2 of the book argued for ethics to be included in the curriculum for nursing and social work education. This is because nursing and social work students need to develop knowledge required for dealing with ethical dilemmas; gain knowledge of how to handle conflict that may arise in the relationship with other professionals and deliver culturally competent services to their increasingly diverse patients and clients groups respectively. The book warned that without ethical education nurses and social workers may not be able to develop capacity to act ethically when confronted with ethical problems during practice. Furthermore, the book argued that the duty to act ethically in nursing and social work practice is a more cogent reason to support ethical education. To advance this argument, chapter 3 of the book demonstrated that nursing and social work practice are moral activities aimed at creating moral goods. Nurses and social workers have moral obligations to protect vulnerable people; assess potential risks to those in their care; act as the patients' or clients' advocate; empower those in care and work within ethical standards and laws.

As ethical theories and ethical principles are the foundations of ethical analysis and guide ethical decision-making, chapter 4 and 5 of the book discussed relevant ethical theories: deontology, consequentialism and virtue; and principles: autonomy, beneficence, non-malficence and justice. This is to advanced the knowledge that ethical theory must be directed towards a universal set of goals and that ethical principles are the universal goals that each theory tries to achieve in order to be successful in ethical decision making (Rainbow, 2002). As ethical principles have the tendency to conflict and give rise to ethical dilemmas, chapter 5 proposed the use of a model and used discussions based on case studies to illustrate conflicts and application of principles or legal obligations that take precedence over others.

In addition to conflicting ethical principles, refusing to give consent, agreeing in the best interest of patient or client, giving information, and balancing the needs of patient or client against those of others and equitable distribution of services and resources often transform into ethical dilemmas. Chapter 6 of this book discussed how the issues could give rise to dilemmas in nursing and social work practice. The book shared the view that successful resolution of ethical dilemmas would depend on the decision maker's logical approach and the process used to resolve the ethical dilemma. Thus, Chapter 7 of the book discussed the importance of developing moral reasoning ability, which is crucial for handling ethical dilemma and making ethical decisions in nursing and social work practice. The principles, value, and legal based approaches to moral reasoning were discussed. The chapter also used discussions based on case studies to illustrate how the approaches inform practice and allow one to make decisions that are morally justifiable.

As much as it is important to develop moral reasoning ability, which is crucial for handling ethical dilemmas and making ethical decisions in nursing and social work practice, chapter 8 discussed the values of models and encouraged the use of models as another form of ethical decision-making paradigms. The chapter drew from the work of many scholars who have written on ethical decision-making models in the design of a simple model to help students gain the knowledge of ethical analysis and ethical decision making. The chapter also used discussions based on case studies to illustrate use of the model in ethical decision-making.

The knowledge of ethics and ethical decision making are essential for nursing and social work professional practice. Yet there are many areas of the subject not covered in this book and other areas requiring further study and publication. An introductory book such as this can only proffer an overview of this vast and exciting subject of ethics. The book focuses only on areas of the subject concerned with ethical decision-making. However, related areas such as those that apply ethical principles to inter-professional working as it relates to decision making have not been covered. This is because there is paucity of research literature relevant to the subject area. The importance of the subject area could be seen from the changing attitude towards a more equitable relationship between the professionals and those in their care. This has subsequently led to changing professional roles, which are giving rise to uncertainties and a potential for conflict of roles. Thus, we are calling for further research to consider the implications of professional caring for an individual nurse or social worker working as part of a team, examine principles and professional guidelines and how these can be used to guide decision making in practice and in professional relationships.

Finally, we hope that our readers have found this book insightful into how nurses and social work students can make sound decisions based on ethical knowledge. Furthermore, we suggest that upon registration for professional practice, the students should continue to reflect on the knowledge gained from reading this book as part of their continuing professional development. This is particularly important as ethics underpins most things they will have to do in their professional practising life.

Bibliography

Abram, L. S. and Moio, J. A. (2009), Critical race theory and the cultural competence dilemma in social work education, *Journal of Social Work Education*, 45 (2), 245-261.

American Nurses Association (ANA) (2011), *Code of ethics for nursing*, *http://nursingworld.org/MainMenuCategories/EthicsStandards/ CodeofEthicsforNurses.aspx* (online access 10 June 2011)

Anscombe, G. E. M. (1958), 'Modern moral philosophy'. *Philosophy*, 33 (124), 1-19.

Anscombe, G. E. M., (1997), Modern moral philosophy in *Virtue Ethics*, Crisp, R. and Slote, M. (Eds), pp. 26-44. Oxford: Oxford University Press.

Aristotle (2002). *Nicomachean Ethics*, translated by Christopher Rowe. Oxford: Oxford University Press.

Armstrong A. (2006), 'Towards a strong virtue ethics for nursing practice' Nursing Philosophy, Volume 7, Issue 3, pages 110-124 *www.ncbi.nlm.nih.gov/pubmed/16774598* (online access 7 June 2011)

Armstrong, A. (2007), *Nursing Ethics: A Virtue-Based Approach*. Palgrave: Macmillan.

Arries, E. (2005), 'Virtue ethics: An approach to moral dilemmas in nursing', *Curationis*, 28 (3), 64-72. *http://www.ncbi.nlm.nih.gov/ pubmed/16245481* (online access 2 April 2011).

Athanassoulis, N. (2004), *Ethics* [Internet Encyclopedia of Philosophy], Keele University, United Kingdom, *http://www.iep.utm.edu/ethics*, (online access 4 December 2009).

Atwal, A. and Jones, M. (2007), 'The importance of the multidisciplinary team', *British Journal of Healthcare Assistants*, Vol **01** No **09**. 387

Baillie, L., Gallagher, A. and Wainwright, P. (2008) *Defending Dignity: Challenges and Opportunities for Nursing*. London: Royal College of Nursing.

Baldwin, T. (2004), *G. E. Moore*, Stanford Encyclopedia of Philosophy, *http://plato.stanford.edu/entries/moore/* (online access 2 April 2011).

Ballet, J. and Bazin, D. (2004), 'Business ethics and ethics of care', *Zagred International Review of Economic and Business*, 7 (2), pp. 43-54.

Banks, S. (1995), *Ethics and Values in Social Work*. London: Macmillan Publishers.

Banks, S. (1998), 'Professional ethics in social work: What future?' *British Journal of Social Work*, 28, 213-231 *http://bjsw.oxfordjournals. org/content/28/2/213.full.pdf* (online access 20 July 2010)

Banks, S. (2001), *Ethics and Values in Social Work*, 2nd edition. London: Palgrave.

Banks, S. (2003), 'From oaths to rulebooks: A critical examination of codes of ethics for the social professions'. *European Journal of Social Work*, 6, pp. 133-144.

Banks, S. and Williams, R. (2005), 'Accounting for ethical difficulties in social welfare work: Issues, problems and dilemmas', *British Journal of Social Work*, 35 (7), pp. 1005-22.

BBC (2008) *Girl Wins Right to Refuse Heart, http://news.bbc.co.uk/1/ hi/england/hereford/worcs/7721231.stm* (online access 18 October 2010).

Beauchamp, T. L. and Childress, J. F. (1994), *Principles of Biomedical Ethics*, 4th edition. New York: Oxford University Press.

Beauchamp, T. L. and Childress, J. F. (2001), *Principles of Biomedical Ethics*, 5th edition. New York: Oxford University Press.

Beauchamp, T. L. and Childress, J. F. (2003), *Principles of Biomedical Ethics*. New York: Oxford University Press.

Beauchamp, T. L. (2008), 'The principle of beneficence in applied ethics', *The Stanford Encyclopedia of Philosophy*, fall 2008. edition, http://plato.   stanford.edu/archives/fall2008/entries/ principle-beneficence/ (online access 16 July 2009).

Beauchamp, T. L. and Childress, J. F. (2009), *Principles of Biomedical Ethics*. New York: Oxford University Press.

Bergum, V. (2002), 'Beyond the rights: The ethical challenge', *Phenomenology Pedagogy*, 10, pp. 53-74. *www.phenomenologyonline. com* (online access 6 August 2010).

Benjamin, M. and Curtis, J. (1992), *Ethics in Nursing*, 3rd edition. Oxford: Oxford University Press.

Benjamin, A. and Templin, J. D. (2003), *Learn the Secret of Legal Reasoning*, *http://www.lawnerds.com/guide/rules.html#TheRuleofLaw* (online access 7 May 2011).

Bernstein, R. (2000), *Books of the Times: Boys, Not Girls, as Society's Victims*, *www.nytimes.com/2000/07/31* (online access 3 April 2010).

Birmingham City University (2005), *Department of Practice Learning*. Birmingham: Birmingham city faculty of health, http://www. health. uce.ac.uk (online access 24 May 2009).

BMA (2000), *Advance Statements About Medical Treatment: Code of Practice*. British Medical Association, London.

BMA (2001), *Consent, Rights and Choices in Health Care for Children and Young People*, British Medical Association.

BMA, RC (UK) and RCN (2001), *Guidance on Legal and Ethical Standards for Planning Patient Care and Decision Making in Relation to Cardiopulmonary Resuscitation*, www.bma.org.uk/ethics/cardio pulmonary_resuscitation/CPRDecisions07.jsp (online access 25 July 2009).

Boland, K. (2006), *Ethical Decision-Making Among Hospital Social Workers*, *http://www.socialworker.com/jswve/content/view/27/44/* (online access 4 October 2010).

Bommer, M., Gratto, C., Gravander, J., and Tuttle, M. (1991), "A behavioral model of ethical decision making', in *Ethical Issues in Information Systems*, R. Dejoie, G. Fowler, and D. Paradice (eds). Boston, MA: Boyd and Fraser Publishing Company.

Borade, G. (2010), *Difference between Ethics and Morality, www.buzzle. com/articles/difference-between-ethics-and-morality.html* (online access 5 April 2010).

Bosshard, G., Broeckaert, B., Clark, D., Materstvedt, L. J, Gordijn, B., and Müller-Busch, H. C. (2008), 'A role for doctors in assisted dying? An analysis of legal regulations and medical professional positions in six European countries', *Journal of Medical Ethics*, 34, pp. 28-32.

Bourdeaux, L., Matthews, L., Richards, N. L., San-Agustin, G., Thomas, P., and Veltigian, S. (2005), 'Comparative study of case management program for patients with syncope', *Journal of Nursing Care Quality*, 20 (2), pp. 140-144.

Bowcott, O. (2009), *Chemical Restraints Killing Dementia Patients http://www.guardian.co.uk/society/2009/nov/12/anti-psychotic-drugs-kill-dementia-patients* (online access 6 April 2009).

Bowles, W., Collingride, M., Curry, S., and Valentine, B. (2006), *Ethical Practice in Social Work*. England: Open University Press.

Braye, S., Preston-Shoot, M., Cull, L., Johns, R., and Roche, J. (2005), *Teaching, Learning, and Assessment of Law in Social Work Educationhttp://www.scie.org.uk/publications/knowledgereviews/kro8.pdf* (online access 12 November 2010).

Brian, O. (2008), The Teaching of Moral Value *www.vision.org/visionmedia/article.aspx?id=6064* (online access 8 February 2010).

Buckley, W. R. and Okrent, C. J. (2004), *Tort and Personal Injury Law*. Clifton Park, New York: Delmar Learning.

Bunnin, N. and Yu, J. (2004), *Analytic Ethics: The Blackwell Dictionary of Western Philosophy*, *www.blackwellreference.com/public/book?id=g9781405106795* (online access 31 March 2011).

Burnard, P. and Chapman, C. (2003), *Professionals and Ethical Issues in Nursing*, 3rd edition. London: Scutari Press.

Carbo, T. and Almagno, S. (2001), "Information ethics: The duty, privilege, and challenge of educating information professionals (at the University of Pittsburgh)', *Library Trends*, 49 (3), pp. 510-518

Carter, L. (2002), *Major Ethical Theories*, Office of Public Policy and Ethics, Institute for Molecular Bioscience; The University of Queensland, Australia *www.uq.edu.au/oppe/PDFS/Ethics_primer.pdf* (online access 9 June 2011)

Castledine, G. (1996), 'Nursing elderly people with dignity and respect', *British Journal of Nursing*, February, 08 (2), http://www.internurse.com/cgi-bin/go.pl/library/abstract.html?uid=6189 (online access 14 July 2009).

Chally, P. (1998), 'Ethics in the trenches: Decision making in practice', *American Journal of Nursing*, 98 (6), pp. 17-20.

Children Act (1989), *Parental Responsibility*, Government Stationary Office,*http://www.legislation.gov.uk/ukpga/1989/41/contents*(online access 8 September 2010).

Citizen Advisory Bureau (2010), *Children and Local Authority Care*, *www.adviceguide.org.uk/index/your_family/family/children_and_local_authority_care.htm* (online access 20 January 2010).

CLA (2008), *Welfare Benefits: Your Right*, *www.communitylegaladvice.org.uk/media/5EC/B8/leaflet09.pdf* (online access 20 January 2010).

Clack, C. (2000), *Social Work Ethics*. London: Palgrave.

Clifford, D. and Burke, B. (2005), 'Developing anti-oppressive ethics in the new curriculum', *Social Work Education*, 24 (6), pp. 677-692.

Cline, A. (2009), *VirtueEthics/EthicalSystemshttp://atheism.about.com/od/ethicalsystems/a/virtueethics.htm*, (online access 26 October 2009). Cline, A. (2011), *Virtue Ethic: Morality and Character http://atheism.about. com/od/ethicalsystems/a/virtueethics.htm*, (online access 15 June 2011).

Cline, A. (2011), Descriptive Ethics: What are our ethical values? *http://atheism.about.com/library/FAQs/phil/blfaq_phileth_desc. htm* (online access 15 June 2011).

Cline, A. (2011), Descriptive, *Normative and Analytic Ethics: Categorizing Ethics & Morality, http://atheism.about.com/library/FAQs/phil/ blfaq_phileth_cat.htm*, (online access 15 June 2011).

Cody, W. K. (2003), Paternalism in nursing and healthcare: central issues and their relation to theory, *Nursing Science Quarterly*: October; 16(4):288-96.

Cohen, Jeryl S. and Erickson, Jeanne M. (2006), Ethical dilemmas and moral distress in oncology nursing practice, *Clinical Journal of Oncology Nursing*

Collins, A. C. (2005), *The Importance of Cultural Competency in Community Health Nursing, www.apha.org/membergroups/ newsletters/ sectionnewsletters/health* (online access 20 April 2011).

Collins English Dictionary (2009), *Ethics Definition.* HarperCollins Publishers, http://www.collinslanguage.com (online access 20 April 2009).

Cox, C. (2001), 'The legal challenges facing nursing', *Journal of Orthopaedic Nursing*, 5 (2), pp. 65-72.

Coughlin, S. S. (2006), *Ethical Issues in Epidemiologic Research and Public Health Practice, http://www.ete-online.com/content/3/1/16* (online access 13 November 2010).

Crain, W. C. (1985), *Theories of Development* (2nd revised edition). New York: Prentice-Hall.

Cribb, A. (2007), 'The ethical dimension: Nursing practice, nursing philosophy and nursing ethics', in J. Tingle and A. Cribb (eds) *Nursing, Law, and Ethics*, 3rd edition. Oxford: Blackwell Publishing, pp. 20-31.

Crisp, R. (1998), 'Modern moral philosophy and the virtues', in *How Should One Live? Essays on the Virtues*, Roger Crisp (Ed.). Oxford: Oxford University Press, 1-18.

CTAD (1998), *Advance Health and Social Care*. Great Clarendon Street, Oxford: Oxford University Press.

Cullity, G. (2004), 'Sympathy, discernment, and reasons', *Philosophy and Phenomenological Research*, 68 (1), pp. 37-62.

Cuthbert, S. and Quallington, J. (2008), *Value for Care Practice*. Devon: Reflect Press Limited.

CQC (2009), *New Registration System: Who Needs to Register? http://www.cqc.org.uk/guidanceforprofessionals/registration*   (online access 11 November 2009).

Denise, T. C., Peterfreund, S. P., and White, N. P. (1999), *Great Traditions in Ethics*, 9th edition. Belmont, CA: Wadsworth Publishing Company.

Deutsch, M. (2000), *'Justice and Conflict', in the Handbook of Conflict Resolution: Theory and Practice*, M. Deutsch and P. T. Coleman (Eds). San Francisco: Jossey-Bass Inc. Publishers, p. 43.

Dickson, J. (2010), *Interpretation and Coherence in Legal Reasoning*, Stanford Encyclopedia of Philosophy. *http://plato.stanford.edu/entries/legal-reas-interpret* (online access 5 October 2010)

Diggory, P. and Judd, M. (2000), 'Advance directives: questionnaire survey of NHS trusts', *British Medical Journal*, 320 (7226), pp. 24-25.

Dimitra, G. (2009), *The Meaning of Ethics and Ethical Dilemmas in Social Work Practice: A Qualitative Study of Greek Social Workers*, A thesis submitted for the degree of Master of Philosophy, United Kingdom, Brunel University,.

Dimond, B. (2001), *Patients' Rights, Responsibilities and the Nurse*, 2nd edition. London Cavendish Publishing Limited.

Dimond, B. (2003), *Legal Aspects of Consent.* Wiltshire: Cromwell Press.

Dimond, B. (2005), *Legal Aspects of Nursing*, 4th edition. Harlow: Pearson education Limited.

Dimond, B. (2008), *Legal Aspects of Nursing*, 5th edition. Harlow: Pearson Education Limited.

Dingwall, L. (2007), 'Medication issues for nursing older people', *Nursing Older People* 19 (2), pp. 32-36.

Directgov (2011), *Your right to refuse future medical treatment, http://www.direct.gov.uk/en/Governmentcitizensandrights/Death/Preparation/DG_10029429*, (online access 3 August 20011)

Dodd, S. and Jansson, B. (2004), 'Expanding the boundaries of ethics education: Preparing social workers for ethical advocacy in an organizational setting', *Journal of Social Work Education*, 40 (3), pp. 455-465.

DOH (2000), *Resuscitation Policy: Health Service Circular HSC 2000/028.* London: Department of Health.

DOH (2000), *Patient Charter,* www.pfc.orq.uk. (online access 28 January 2009).

DOH and Home Office (2001), *Seeking Consent: Working with Children* www.dh.gov.uk/en/Publicationsandstatistics/Publications/ PublicationspolicyAndGuidance/DH_4007005 (online access 20 April 2009).

DOH (2004), *The NHS Improvement Plan.* United Kingdom: Department of Health, The Stationery Office (TSO).

DOH (2005), *Mental Capacity Act,* *www.dh.gov.uk/en/ SocialCare/Deliveringadultsocialcare/Mental*Capacity/ MentalCapacityAct2005/DH_073511 (access 14 April 2009)

DOH (2006a), *Our Health, Our Care, Our Say: A New Direction for Community Services.* Her Majesty's Stationery Office (HMSO).

DOH (2006a), *Modeling Nursing Careers: Setting the Direction.* London: Department of Health.

DOH (2006b), *Learning for a Change in Healthcare.* Her Majesty's Stationery Office (HMSO).

DOH (2009), *Reference Guide to Consent for Examination or Treatment,* 2nd edition, *www.dh.gov.uk/prod/consumdh/groups/dhdigitalasset/ dh 103653.pdf,* (online access 10 December 2009).

Dolgoff, R., Loewenberg, F. M., and Harrington, D. (2005), *Ethical Decisions for Social Work Practice,* 7th edition. Belmont, CA: Brooks/ Cole.

Drennan, M. (2003), *Concord http://www.fs.gov.za/Departments/SAC/ Library/Depart/language_articles.htm* (online access 21 December 2010).

Dunn, M. (1998), '*Knowledge helps health care professionals deal with ethical dilemmas*', *AORN,* 67 (3), pp. 658-661, *www.ScienceDirect. com,science* (online access 4 December 2009).

ECHR (2004), *H.L. v. The United Kingdom—45508/99, ECHR 471* (5 October 2004), European Court of Human Rights, *http://www.bailii. org/eu/cases/ECHR/2004/471.html,* (online access 3 August 2011)

Eckberg, E. (1998), 'The continuing ethical dilemma of the do-not-resuscitate order', *AORN Journal, http://findarticles.com/p/ articles/mi_moFSL,* (online access 28 December 2009).

Edwards, S. D. (1996), *Nursing Ethics.* Hampshire: Basingstoke, United Kingdom: Palgrave Macmillan Limited,

Edwards, S. D. (2009), *Nursing Ethics: A Principle-Based Approach*, 2nd edition. Basingstoke, United Kingdom: Palgrave Macmillan Limited.

Ellis, P. (2006), *Exploring the concept of acting 'in the Patients' best interest'*, *http://www.internurse.com/cgi-bin/go.pl/library/article.cgi? uid=9975;article=BJN_5_17_1072_1074*, (online access 25 July 2011).

Encyclopedia Britannica (2010), *History and Society: Ethics, http://www.britannica.com/EBchecked/topic/194023/ethics* (online access 17 July 2010).

Fallat, M. E. and Deshpande, J. K. (2004), 'Do-not-resuscitate orders for pediatric patients who require anesthesia and surgery', *Pediatrics*, 114 (6), *http://aappolicy.aappublications.org/cgi/reprint/pediatrics;114/6/1686.pdf* (online access 28 March 2011).

Family Reform Act (1969), *Stationery Office and Queen's Printer of Acts of Parliament, www.uk-legislation.hmso.gov.uk/acts/acts1969/pdf* (online access 8 September 2010).

Faunce, T. A. (2004), 'Developing and teaching the virtue-ethics foundations of healthcare whistle blowing', *Monash Bioethics Review*, 23 (4), pp. 41-55.

Feather, N. T. (2002), 'Values and value dilemmas in relation to judgments concerning outcomes of an industrial conflict', *Personality and Social Psychology Bulletin*, 28 (4), pp. 446-458.

Field, L. and Smith, B. (2008), *Nursing Care: An Essential Guide*. Harlow: Pearson Education Ltd.

Fieser, J. (2007), *Normative Ethics*, Internet Encyclopedia of Philosophy, *www.iep.utm.edu/normative* (online access 2 April, 2010).

Fieser, J. (2009), *Ethics [Internet Encyclopedia of Philosophy]*, University of Tennessee at Martin, *http://www.iep.utm.edu/ethics*, (online access 2 April, 2010).

Fitzpatrick, J. J. (2007), Cultural Competence in Nursing Education Revisited, *http://findarticles.com/p/articles/mi_hb3317/is_1_28/ai_n29325824/* (online access 10 June 2011).

Foley, B. J. (2009), 'The nature of advocacy vs. paternalism in nursing: Clarifying the "thin line"', *Journal of Advanced Nursing*, 8, pp.1746-1752.

Forester-Miller, H. F. and Davis, T. (1996), *A Practitioner's Guide to Ethical Decision Making*. Alexandria, VA: American Counseling Association.

Foster, L., Sharp, J., Scesny, A., McLellan, L., and Cotman, K. (1993), 'Bioethics: Social work's response and training needs', *Social Work in Health Care*, **19** (1), pp. 15-39.

Fletcher, L. and Buka, P. (1999), *A Legal Framework for Caring*. Basingstoke, United Kingdom: Palgrave

Foster, C. (2007), 'Negligence—A legal perspective', in Tringle, J. and Cribb, A. (Eds), *Nursing Law and Ethics*, 3rd edition, Oxford: Blackwell Publishing Ltd

Fraser, K. D. and Strang, V. (2004), 'Decision-making and nurse case management. A philosophical perspective', *Advances in Nursing Science*, 27 (1), pp. 32-43.

Fry, S. (2008), *Ethics in Nursing Practice*, 3rd edition. Chichester, United Kingdom: Wiley-Blackwell:

Fry, S. and Johnstone, M. (2008), *Ethics in Nursing Practice: A Guide to Making Ethical Decisions*, 3rd edition. Oxford: Blackwell Publishing.

Fry, H., Ketteridge, S. and Marshall, S. (1999), *A Handbook for Teaching and Learning in Higher Education*. Glasgow: Kogan Page.

Galambos, C., Watt, W., Anderson, K., Danis, F. (2006), *Ethics Forum: Rural Social Work Practice: Maintaining Confidentiality in the Face of Dual Relationships*, www.socialworker.com/jswve edn (online access 29 January 2009)

Garret, J. (2005), *Virtue Ethics: A Basic Introductory Essay, http://www. wku.edu/~jan.garrett/ethics/virtthry.htm#q6*, (online access 26 October 2009).

Gass, W. H., (1957), The case of the obliging stranger', *The Philosophical Review*, 66, pp. 193-204.

Gastmans, C. (1999), 'Care as a moral attitude in nursing', *Nursing Ethics*, 6 (214), http://nej.sagepub.com/content/6/3/214.full. pdf+html (Online Access, 7 April 2011).

General Medical Council (2008), *Withholding and Withdrawing Life Prolonging Treatments: Good Practice in Decision Making, www. gmcuk.org/guidance/current/library* (online access 20 July 2009).

Gerard, K., (2002), The importance of nursing values in inter professional collaboration', *British Journal of Nursing*, 11 (1) 65-68.

Gert, B. (2008), 'The definition of morality', *Stanford Encyclopedia of Philosophy, www.seop.leeds.ac.uk/entries/morality-definition* (online access 5 April 2010).

Gibbons, P. (2008), 'Ethical dimensions of practice', in Hincliff, S., Norman, S., and Schober, J. (Eds), *Nursing Practice and Healthcare: A Foundation Text*, 5th edition. London: Edward Arnold Ltd, p. 179. Gilligan, C. (1977), *'In a different voice: Women's conceptions of self and morality'*, *Harvard Educational Review*, 47 (4). Gilligan, C. (1982), *In a Different Voice: Psychological Theory and Women's Development*. Cambridge, MA: Harvard University Press. Gillon R. (1994), 'Medical ethics: Four principles plus attention to scope', *British Medical Journal* 309, pp. 184-188.

Gillon, R. (2003), 'Ethics needs principles—four can encompass the rest—and respect for autonomy should be "first among equals"', *Journal of Medical Ethics*, 29, pp. 307-312.

Grace, P. J. (2001), 'Professional advocacy: Widening the scope of accountability', *Nursing Philosophy*, 2, pp. 151-162.

Grace, P. J. (2008), *Nursing Ethics and Professional Responsibility in advanced practice.* Sudbury, MA: Jones and Bartlett.

Griffith, R. and Tengnah, C. (2008), *Law and Professional Issues in Nursing*. Exeter: Learning Matters Ltd.

Griffith, R. (2006), 'Tablet crushing: Calls for caution', *Nursing in Practice*, March/April, pp. 49-50.

GMC (1998), *Seeking Patients' Consent: The Ethical Considerations.* London: General Medical Council.

Goff, J. (2011), *Professional Values and Ethics, http://socyberty.com/ philosophy/professional-values-and-ethics* (online access 2 April 2011)

GSCC (2010), *Code of Practice for Social Care Workers*, http://www. gscc.org.uk/cmsFiles/Registration/Codesper   cent20of   per cent20Practice/CodesofPracticeforSocialCareWorkers.pdf (online access 6 June 2011)

Guarisco, K. K. (2004*)*, 'Managing do-not-resuscitate orders in the perianesthesia period', *Journal of Perianesthesia Nursing, http:// www.jopan.org/article/S1089-9472(04)00288-6/abstract*   (online access 28 March 2011)

Guenther, D. (2009), *An Example of a FIRAC Analysis, http:// www.100megsfree3.com/wordsmith/firactermsexample.html* (online access 5 May 2011).

Gunaratnam, Y. (2007), Intercultural palliative care: Do we need cultural competence? *International Journal of Palliative Nursing*, 13

(10), pp. 470-477, *http://www.ncbi.nlm.nih.gov/pubmed/18073705* (online access 10 June 2011)

Haidt, J. *(2001), The emotional dog and its rational tail: A social intuitionist approach to moral judgment. Psychological Review. 108, 814-834*

Harrison, J. (2001), *The Value Of Life—An Introduction to Medical Ethics.* New York: Routledge and Kegan Paul, pp 1-6.

Hartsell, B. D. (2006), 'A model for ethical decision-making: The Context of Ethics', *Journal of Social Work Values and Ethics http://www.socialworker.com/jswve/content/view/26/44/* (online access 8 March 2011).

Hawley, G. (2007), *Ethics in Clinical Practice: An Interprofessional Approach:* Pearson Education

Hayes, A. (2010), *Types of Moral Philosophy, http://www.ehow.com/about_5415224_types-moral-philosophy.html* (online access 17 July 2010)

Hendrick, J. (2001), *Law and ethics in nursing and health care.* United Kingdom: Nelson Thornes.

Hendrick, J. (2004), *Law and Ethics, Foundations in Nursing and Health Care.* Cheltenham: Nelson Thornes Ltd.

Henry S. Richardson (2007), *Moral Reasoning,* Stanford Encyclopedia of Philosophy, *http://plato.stanford.edu/entries/reasoning-moral/#1,* (online access 4 November 2009)

Herring, J. (2006), *Medical Law and Ethics.* New York: Oxford University Press.

Herring, J. (2008), *Medical Law and Ethics.* New York: Oxford University Press

Hindson, E. and Caner, E. (2008), *The Popular Encyclopedia of Apologetics: Surveying the Evidence for the truth of Christians.* Oregan: Harvest House Publishers.

Hoagland, S. L. (1990), Some Concerns about Nel Nodding, *Caring Hypatia* 5 (1).

Homemoral (2007), *Ethicaldilemmainnursing.http://www.homemorals.com/ethical-dilemma/ethical-dilema-In-nursing.html* (online access 19 November 2009)

Hope, Savulescu and Hendrick (2003), *Medical Ethics and Law: The Core Curriculum.* Churchill Livingstone

Hugman, R. (2005), *New Approaches in Ethics for the Caring Profession.* Palgrave, Macmillan.

Hull, L., Dolan, A and Newling, D. (2007), *Jehovah's Witness mother dies after refusing blood transfusion after giving birth to twins*, *http://www.dailymail.co.uk/news/article-491791/Jehovahs-Witness-mother-dies-refusing-blood-transfusion-giving-birth-twins.html#ixzz1UFGQEa3G* (online access 5 August 2011)

Hursthouse, R. (1999), *Introduction In Virtue Ethics.* Oxford: Oxford University Press.

Hursthouse, R. (2007), *Virtue Ethics, Stanford Encyclopedia of Philosophy. http://www.science.uva.nl/~seop/archives/win2008/entries/ethics-virtue* (online access 20 November 2010)

Iacovino, L. (2002), "Ethical principles and information professionals: theory, practice, and education," *Australian Academic and Research Libraries*, Vol. 33 No.2, pp. 57-74.

ICN (2009), *About ICN: The International Council of Nurses, http://www.icn.ch/abouticn.htm,* (online access 11 November 2009) Independent News Online (1993), *Jehovah's Witness died after refusing blood transfusion*, Friday, 8 January 1993 *www.independent.co.uk/news/uk/jehovahs-witness-dies-afterrefusing-blood-transfusion-1477165.html* (online access 20 December 2011)

IFSW and IASSW (2004), *International Federation of Social Workers (IFSW), International Association of Schools of Social Work (IASSW), http://www.ifsw.org/p38000040.html,* (online access 10 November 2009)

IFSW and IASSW (2005), *International Federation of Social Workers (IFSW), International Association of Schools of Social Work (IASSW), Ethics in Social Work, Statement of Principles, http://www.ifsw.org/f38000032.html,* (online access 7 April 2011)

Illingsworth, S. (2004), *Approach to Ethics in higher education*, PRS-LTSN, *www.prs-ltsn.ac.uk/ethics* (online access 29 January 2009).

International Federation of Social Workers (2005), *Ethics in Social Work, Statement of Principles.* http://www.ifsw.org/en/f38000032.html. (online access 29 January 2009)

Jackson, E. (2006), *Medical Law: Text, Cases and Materials*, 1st edition, Oxford: Oxford University Press.

Joffe S, Manocchia M,Weeks J. C., Clear, PD (2003),What do patients value in their hospital care? An empirical perspective on autonomy-centred bioethics. *Journal of Medical Ethics* 29: 103-8

Johnstone, M. J. (1999), *Bioethics: A nursing perspective*, 3rd edition. Saunders, Marrickville, NSW.

Joseph, M. V. and Conrad, A. P. (1989), Social work influence on interdisciplinary ethical decision-making in health care settings. *Health and Social Work, 14*, (1) 22-30.

Joseph Walsh; Rosemary Farmer; Melissa Floyd Taylor; Kia J. Bentley (2004), Ethical dilemma of practicing social workers around psychiatric medication, *Social Work in Mental Health*, 1533-2993, Volume 1, Issue 4

Kant, Immanuel (1964), *Groundwork of the Metaphysics of Morals*, in Trans. H. J. Paton New York: Harper and Row.

Kathleen M. Foley and Herbert Hendin (2002), *The case against assisted suicide: for the right to end-of-life care*, The John Hokins University Press

Kennedy, I. (2003), Patients are experts in their own field. *British Medical Journal (BMJ)* 326: 1276-7

Kennedy, W. (2004), Beneficence and autonomy in nursing (2004, *British Journal of Perioperative Nursing, 14* (11), pp. 500-506.

Kevin, T. (2007), *Moral Character*, Internet Encyclopedia of Philosophy, *http://www.iep.utm.edu/moral-ch/*, (online access 10 November 2009).

Knowledgerush (2009), *descriptive ethics, www.knowledgerush.com/ kr/encyclopedia* (online access 5 April 2010)

Kohlberg, L. (1971), *"Stages in Moral Development as a Basis for Moral Education."* In C. M. Beck, B. S. Crittenden, and E. V. Sullivan, Eds. *Moral Education: Interdisciplinary Approaches*. Toronto: Toronto University Press.

Kohlberg, L. (1971), *From* Is *to* Ought*: How to Commit the Naturalistic Fallacy and Get Away with It in the Study of Moral Development*. New York: Academic Press.

Kohlberg, L. (1973), The Claim to Moral Adequacy of a Highest Stage of Moral Judgment, *Journal of Philosophy* 70: 630-646.

Kohlberg, L., Lickona, T. (1976), moral stages and moralization: The cognitive-developmental approach, Moral Development and Behaviour*: Theory, Research and Social Issues*. Holt, New York: Rinehart and Winston.

Kraut, R. (2010), *Aristotelian Ethics*, Stanford Encyclopedia of Philosophy, *http://plato.stanford.edu/entries/aristotle-ethics*, (online access 7 June 2011).

Kugelman-Jaffee, W. (1990), *Ethical decision-making of social work practitioners in organizational settings*. Unpublished doctoral dissertation. City University of New York.

Kurtis Karr (2009), *Ethical Dilemma Facts, www.morally.net/Ethical_ dilemma/encyclopedia.htm* (online access, 15 November 2009)

Lark, J and Gatti, C. (1999), *Compliance with Advance Directives*: Nursing's View, Critical Care Nursing Quarterly, Volume 22, Number 3, pages 65-71, *http://www.nursingcenter.com/library/ JournalArticle. asp?Article_ID=437841* (online access 28 July 2010)

Leadbetter, M. (2002), 'Empowerment and Advocacy' in Adams, R., Dominelli, L. and Payne, M. (eds) *Social Work: Themes, Issues and Critical Debates*, Basingstoke, Palgrave in association with the Open University.

Leathard, A. and McLaren, S. (2007), *ethics contemporary challenges in health and social care.* Bristol: The Policy press.

Leishman, J. (2004), Perspectives of cultural competence in health care, *Nursing Standard*, RCN Publishing, Harrow, vol. 19, n°11, pp. 33-38

Lin, Y. H., Wang, L. S., Yarbrough, S., Alfred, S. and Martin, P. (2010), Changes in Taiwanese Nursing student values during educational experience, *Nursing Ethics*, August 27, vol. 17no. 5 646-654

Lloyd, L (2006), *A Caring Profession? The Ethics of Care and Social Work with Older People*, British Journal of Social Work (7):1171-85; doi:10.1093/ bjsw/bch4 *http://bjsw.oxfordjournals.org/cgi/content/ full/36/7/1171* (online access 28 July 2010)

Loewenberg, F. and Dolgoff, R. (1992) (4th edition), *Ethical Decisions for Social Work Practice* F. E. Peacock Publishers, Inc., Itasca, Illinois.

Loewenberg, F. and Dolgoff, R. (1996), *Ethical decisions for social work practice.* Itasca, Illinois: F. E. Peacock Publishers.

Long, L. and Roche, J. (2001), *The Law and Social Work:* Contemporary Issues for Practice, Palgrave Macmillan

Lorenzetti, J. P. (2010), *Ethical Frameworks for Academic Decision-Making http://www.facultyfocus.com/articles/faculty-development/ethical- frameworks-for-academic-decision-making* (online access 30 April 2010)

Lowden, J. (2002), Children's rights: a decadeof dispute, *Journal of Advanced Nursing* 37: 100-7

Luce, J. M. (1997), Withholding and withdrawal of life support from critically ill patients. *Western Journal of Medicine, 167: 411-416.*

Ludwick, R., Silva, M. C. (2000), *"Ethics: Nursing Around the World: Cultural Values and Ethical Conflicts"* Online Journal of Issues in Nursing Vol. 5 No. 3 Available: *www.nursingworld.org/ MainMenuCategories/ANAMarketplace/ANAPeriodicals/OJIN/*

Columns/Ethics/CulturalValuesandEthicalConflicts.aspx (online access 12 June 2011)

MacDonald C. (2010), *A Guide to Moral Decision Making, http://www. ethicsweb.ca/guide/guide2010.pdf* (online access 24 March 2011)

MacDonald, H. (2007), Relational ethics and advocacy in nursing: literature review. *Journal of Advanced Nursing* 57(2), 119-126 doi: 10.1111/j.1365-2648.2006.04063.x

Maiese, Michelle (2003), *"Distributive Justice." Beyond Intractability.* Eds. Guy Burgess and Heidi Burgess. Conflict Research Consortium, University of Colorado, Boulder. Posted: June 2003 http://www. beyondintractability.org/essay/distributive_justice, (online access 8 November 2010).

Malcolm, P. (2007), *Know your colleagues: Role of social worker in end-of-life care, End of Life Care,* Vol. 1, No. 1, *http://endoflifecare. co.uk/journal/0101_colleagues.pdf,* (online access 20 January 2010)

Mason J. K. and Laurie G. T. *Mason and McCall Smith's (2006) Law and Medical Ethics,* 7th edition. Oxford: OUP.

Mattison, M. (1994), *Ethical decision-making in social work practice.* Unpublished doctoral dissertation. Columbia University. School of Social Work.

Mattison, M. (2000), Ethical decision-making. The person in process. *Social Work, 45,* (3) 201-212.

Matzo, M. L., Sherman, D. W., Nelson-Marten, P., Rhome, A. and Grant, M. (2004), Ethical and legal issues in end-of-life care: content of the end-of-life nursing education consortium curriculum and teaching strategies. *Journal for Nurses in Staff Development,* 20(2), 59-66

Meagher, G., Parton, N. (2004), *Modernising Social Work and the Ethics of Care. Social Work and Society,* vol.2, www.socwork.de/ Meagher-Parton2004.pdf. (online access 9 November 2008).

MCaulffe, D. (2005), *I Am Still Standing: Impacts and Consequences of Ethical Dilemmas for Social Workers in Direct Practice.* Journal of Social Work Values and Ethics, vol. 2(1), Available from: www. socialworker.com/jswve, (Online access, 29 January 2009).

MCaulffe, D. (2005), Putting Ethics on the Organisational Agenda: The Social Work Ethics Audit on Trial. *Australian Social Work,* 58(4), pp. 357-369.

McBeath, G., Webb, S. A. (2002), Virtue Ethics and Social Work: Being Lucky, Realistic, and not Doing ones duty. *The British Journal of Social Work,* 32(8), pp. 1015-36.

McCloskey, D. (2007), *The Bourgeois Virtues: Ethics for an Age of Commerce.* Chicago: University of Chicago Press. ISBN: 978-0-22655-664-2.

McCormick Thomas R. (2008), *Principles of Bioethics: Ethics in medicine,* University of Washington School of Medicine, *http://depts. washington.edu/bioethx/tools/princpl.html#prin1* (online access 6 September 2010)

McDermott, A. (2002), *Involving patients in discussions of do-not-resuscitate orders, http://www.nursingtimes.net/nursing-practice-clinical-research,* (online access 20 July 2009)

McDonald, H. P. (2001), Toward a Deontological Environmental Ethic, *Environmental Ethics,* 23 (4), 411-430.

McElreath, F. S. (2006), Maximizing Act Consequentialism and Friendship, *The Journal of Value Inquiry* 40:413-420, DOI 10.1007/s10790-007-9011-x *http://www.springerlink.com/content/j2724l106047jrv1/fulltext.pdf* (Online access, 15 April 2011)

McGraw, K. S. (1998), *Should do-not-resuscitate orders be suspended during surgical procedures? AORN Journal, http://findarticles.com/p/articles/mi_moFSL* (online access 28 December 2009)

McHale, J. and Gallagher, A. (2003), *Nursing and Human Rights.* Butterworth Heinemann.

McLean, S. and Mason, J. K. (2003), *Legal and Ethical Aspects of Healthcare,* London, Cromwell Press.

Michael, P., Gwyneth, R. and Stuart, V. (2001), '*Values in social work law: strained relations or sustaining relationships?' Journal of Social Welfare and Family Law,* 23: 1, 1-22, (online access 31 March 2011).

Milberg, A., Strang, P. and Sand, L. (2007), *Dying cancer patients' experiences of powerlessness and helplessness, Support Care Cancer* 16:853-862, DOI 10.1007/s00520-007-0359-z, *http://www.springerlink.com/content/h712425687787488/fulltext.pdf* (online access 31 March 2011)

Mill, J. S. (1998), *Utilitarianism.* Oxford: Oxford University Press. *ISBN 978-0-19-875163-2*

Miller, H. F. and Davis, T. (1996), *A Practitioner's Guide to Ethical Decision Making,* American Counselling Association, *www.counseling.org/Files/FD,* (online access 3 April 2010)

Mintz, S. (2010), *what is ethics?* In Ethics Sage, *http://www.ethicssage.com/2010/12/what-is-ethics.html* (online access 10 June 2011)

Monzon, J. (1999), *Teaching Ethical Issues in Biomedical Engineering,* Int.

J. Engng Ed. Vol. 15, No. 4, pp. 276±281, 1999*http://www.ijee.dit. ie/ articles/Vol15-4/ijee1071.pdf* (online access 16 September 2010) Moonie, N. (2005), *Health and Social Care.* Oxford, United Kingdom: Heinemann educational Nagel, T. (2005), The Problem of Global Justice. *Philosophy and Public Affairs* 33, 113-147.

NASW (2001), *Standard for cultural competence in social work,* National Association of Social Work, *www.socialworkers.org/practice/ standards/NASWCulturalStandards.pdf* (online access 10 June 2011)

NASW (2008), *Code of Ethics of the National Association of Social Workers, http://www.socialworkers.org/pubs/code/code.asp* (online access 6 June 2011)

New World Encyclopedia (2008), *Ethics of Care, http://www. newworldencyclopedia.org/entry/Ethics_of_care,* (online access 28 July 2010)

NHS (2008), *Guidelines for Consent to Treatment of children, www. ndhc.nhs.uk/foi/content/parttwo/class08/docs/ClinGuide/Guidelines* (online access 6 January 2010)

NMC (2004), *Professional code of conduct: standards for conduct, performance and ethics.* Nursing and Midwifery Council, London

NMC (2007), *Professional Code of Conduct,* Nursing and Midwifery Council, London.

NMC (2007), Guidelines: *Covert administration of medicines—disguising medicine in food and drink,* Nursing and Midwifery Council, London.

NMC (2008), *The Code: Standards of Conduct, Performance and Ethics for Nurses and Midwives,* Nursing and Midwifery Council, London.

NMC (2009), *About us, http://www.nmc-uk.org/aSection. aspx?SectionID=5,* (online access 10 November 2009)

NMC (2010), *Standards for pre-registration nursing education:* Nursing and Midwifery Council, London. *http://standards.nmcuk.org/Pages/ Downloads.aspx* (online access 21 September 2010)

Noddings, N. (1984), *Caring: a feminine approach to ethics and moral education* University of California Press, Berkeley.

NOS (2002), *The National Occupational Standards for Social Work, http://www.york.ac.uk/depts/spsw/socialwork/practice/document*

s/3SWNOSdocpdffileseditionApr04.pdf (online access 19 January 2010)

O'Malley Beverly Hansen (2009*), what is an Ethical Dilemma in Nursing Practice?*   *http://www.registered-nurse-canada.com/ethical_ dilemma.html*, (online access 16 September 2010)

Online Encyclopedia (2004), *non-malficence definition*, http://www. encyclo.co.uk/define/nonmaleficence (online access 20 March 2009)

OPSI (1961), *Suicide Act 1961*, available online from: *www.opsi.gov.uk/ RevisedStatutes/Acts/ukpga/1961/cukpga_19610060_en_1* (online access 20 August 2009)

OPSI (1998), *Human Rights Act 1998*, available online from *www.opsi. gov.uk/acts/acts1998/ukpga* (online access 15 July 2009)

OPSI (2005), *Disability Discrimination Act 1995* available online from *www.opsi.gov.uk/acts/acts1995/ukpga*, (online access 10 July 2009)

OPSI (2005), *Children Act 1989* available online from *www.opsi.gov.uk/ acts/acts1995/ukpga*, (online access 12 July 2009).

OPSI (2005), *Mental Capacity Act 2005*. Available online from *www. opsi.gov.uk/acts/acts2005/ukpga* (online access 15 July 2009)

Ord, T. (2005), *Consequentialism and Decision Procedures, http://www. amirrorclear.net/academic/papers/decision-procedures.pdf* (online access 15 April 2011)

Page, J. S. (2008), *Peace Education: Exploring Ethical and Philosophical Foundations.* Charlotte: Information Age Publishing.

Parker, J. (2004), *Effective Practice Learning in Social Work.* Learning Matters Limited, Exeter, United Kingdom.

Parrott, L. (2008), *Values and ethics in social work practice.* Exeter, United Kingdom: Learning Matters Limited.

Parrott, L. (2009), *Constructive marginality: conflicts and dilemmas in cultural competence and anti-oppressive practice*, Social Work Education, 28(6), pp. 617-630, *http://www.scie-socialcareonline. org.uk/profile.asp?guid=1a816d8d-3b0c-4ef0-a112-0303511b33e0* (online access 10 June 2011)

Paton, H. J. (1971), *The Categorical Imperative: A Study in Kant's Moral Philosophy*, Philadelphia: University of Pennsylvania Press.

Paul, R. and Elder, L. (2005), *Foundation for critical thinking, www. criticalthinking.org* (online access 28 September 2010)

Payne, M. (2007), *Know your colleagues: role of social work in end-of-life care*, End of Life Care, Volume 1, No 1. *http://endoflifecare.co.uk/ journal/0101_colleagues.pdf* (Online Access, 23 July 2010)

Penslar, Robin L. (1995), *Research Ethics: Cases and Materials. Bloomington:* Indiana University Press.

Pera, S. A. and Tonder, S. V. (ed.) (2005), *ethics in health care,* 2nd edition. Landsowne: Juta Academic.

Phillips, A. (1979), 'Social work and the delivery of legal services', *Modern Law Review,* no 42, pp 29-41.

Pojman, L. P. and Fieser, J. (2009), Virtue Theory. In *Ethics: Discovering Right and Wrong,* 6th edition. Belmont, CA: Wadsworth.

Povar, G., Blumen, H., Daniel, J., Daub, S., Evans, L., Holm, R. et al (2004), Ethics in practice: Managed care and the changing health care environment. *Academia and Clinic, 141*(2), 131-136.

Schober, J. (eds*.) Nursing Practice and Healthcare, A Foundation Text,* 5th edition. London: Edward Arnold Ltd.

Slote, M. (2001), *Morals from motives.* Oxford, United Kingdom: Oxford University Press.

Smart, J. C. and William, B. (1973), Williams Bernard: "*A Critique of Utilitarianism," in Utilitarianism: For and Against.* Cambridge: Cambridge University Press, 1973.

Torjuul, K., Nordam, A., Sørlie, V. (2005), Action ethical dilemmas in surgery: an interview study of practicing surgeons, *BMC Medical Ethics,* 6:7.

QAA (2000) Subject benchmark statements Social Policy and Administration and Social Work, *www.qaa.ac.uk/ academicinfrastructure/benchmark/honours/socialpolicy* (online access 1 February 2010)

QAA (2008), *Subject benchmark statement, www.qaa.ac.uk/ academicinfrastructure/benchmark/honours/default.asp* (online access 8 April 2010)

Quallington, J. and Cuthbert, S. (2008), *Values for Care Practice,* Hampshire, Reflect Press Limited.

Quinn. A. (2007), *Moral Virtues for Journalists,* Journal of Mass Media Ethics, 22(2and3), 168-186 *http://jcomm.uoregon.edu/~tbivins/ J397/PDFs_F10/Virtues_for_ journalists_(Quinn).pdf* (online access 15 June 2011)

Railton, R. (1984), *Alienation: Consequentialism, and the Demands of Morality Philosophy and Public Affairs,* Vol. 13, No. 2. (Spring), pp. 134-171, *http://philosophy.ucsd.edu/faculty/rarneson/Courses/ railtonalienationconsequentialism.pdf* (Online access, 31 August 2010)

Rainbow, C. (2002), *Descriptions of Ethical Theories and Principles*, *www.bio.davidson.edu/people/kabernd/Indep/carainbow/Theories.htm* (online access 31 August 2010)

Ransome, W. (2010), *Is Agent-Based Virtue Ethics Self-Undermining? Ethical Perspectives 17 www.griffith.edu.au/_data/assets/pdf_file/0010/208738/Self-Undermining.pdf* (online access 31 August 2010)

Reamer F. G. (1982), *Ethical Dilemmas in Social Service.* New York: Columbia University Press.

Reamer, F. (1990), *Ethical dilemmas in social service.* New York: Columbia University Press.

RCN (2003), *Restraining, holding still and containing children and young people: Guidance for nursing staff,* The Royal College of Nursing London.

RCN (2003), *London, Royal College of Nursing,* www.rcn.odata/assets/pdffile/0009/78570/001999.pdf (Online access, 14 July 2009)

RCN (2009), *Letter from the Chair: Professor Paul Wainwright, http://www.rcn.org.uk/development/communities/specialisms/ethics/news_stories/letter_from_the_chair_professor_paul_wainwright_summer_,* (online access 6 June 2011)

RCN (2009), *Transcultural health care practice: Foundation module, www.rcn.org.uk/development/learning/transcultural_health/foundation/sectionthree* (online access 13 June 2011)

Rhode, D. (1992), 'Ethics by the pervasive method', *Journal of Legal Education,* no 42, pp 31-56.

Richardson, H. S. (2007), *Moral Reasoning,* Stanford Encyclopedia of Philosophy, *http://plato.stanford.edu/entries/reasoning-moral,* (online access 28 September 2010)

Ridley, Aaron (1998), *Beginning Bioethics.* New York: St. Martin's Press.

Robert T., Buttram, R. F., and Sheppard, B. H. (1995), *Equity, Equality and Need: Three Faces of Social Justice,* In Conflict, Cooperation, and Justice: Essays Inspired by the Work of Morton Deutsch, eds. B. B. Bunker and Morton Deutsch, San Francisco, Jossey-Bass Inc. Publishers, 261.

Ross, W. D. (1930), *The Right and the Good.* Oxford: Clarendon Press: 26-7 Rumbold, G. (1999), *Ethics in nursing practice,* 3rd edition. Edinburgh: Harcourt brace and company limited.

Rottenstein Law Group, (2011), *What is proximate cause? www.rotlaw.com/legal-resources/causes-of-action/ what-is-proximate-cause* (online access 28 July 2011)

Rumbold, G. (2002), *Ethics in Nursing Practice*. Bailliere Tindall Published in association with RCN.

Sacks, D. (2005), *Ethical and Legal Issues www.healthinaging.org/ agingintheknow/chapters* (online access 15 May 2010)

Sakshi, S. (2010), What are moral values? *http://hubpages.com/hub/ What-are-moral-value* (online access 8 February 2010)

Sarvimaki, A. (2006), *Nursing care as a moral, practical, communicative and creative* activity, *Journal of Advanced Nursing, Volume 13, Issue 4,* 22 DEC 2006, http://onlinelibrary.wiley.com/doi/10.1111/j.1365-2648.1988.tb02850.x/abstract (online access 7 April 2011)

Scheffler, S. (1988), *Consequentialism and Its Critics*. Oxford: Oxford University Press.

Schenck, D. P. (2002), *Ethical consideration in the treatment of head and neck cancer, www.moffitt.org/ccjRoof/v9n5/pdf/410.pdf* (online access 4 December 2009)

Seedhouse, D. (1988) *Ethics: the Heart of Health Care.* Chichester: J Wiley and Sons. Seedhouse, D. (2003) *Ethics: The Heart of Health Care,* 2nd edition. West Sussex: John Wiley and Sons. Shaffer, D. R. (2004), *Social and Personality Development,* 5th edition, Wadsworth Publishing.

Shastri, A. and Wilson, A.J (2001), *The post-colonial states of South Asia: democracy, development, and identity,* Palgrave Macmillan, Shelter (2010), Housing benefit and local housing allowance, *www. shelter.org.uk* (online access 21 January 2010) Sherwin, S. (1992), *No Longer Patient: Feminist Ethics and Healthcare,* Philadelphia: Temple University Press.

Shirey, M. (2005), Ethical climate in nursing practice: The leader's role. *JONA'S Healthcare, Law, Ethics, and Regulation, 7(2),* 59-67.

Slote, M. (2001), *Morals from Motives.* Oxford: Oxford University Press.

Sidgwick, Henry (1907), *The Method of Ethics.* New York: Dover (1981). HYPERLINK "http://en.wikipedia.org/wiki/ Special:BookSources/0915145286" ISBN 0915145286

Simpson, T. (2008), *The Art of Written Persuasion: From IRAC to FAILSAFE—A Compilation of Legal Problem-Solving Models, www. llrx.com/columns/persuasion3.htm* (online access 14 May 2011)

Smith, G. E. (1999), An introduction to health care ethics, *Journal of Radiotherapy in Practice* Vol.1 No. 1 GMM

Smith, G. E. (1999), *Autonomy, paternalism, advocacy and consent,* Journal of Radiotherapy in Practice, http://journals.cambridge.

org/download.php?file=per   cent2FJRPper   cent2FJRP1_03per cent2FS1460396999000242a.pdfandcode=91c4b318bf15e311ead 73b8e039e5e6c (online access 16 June 2011)

Smith, G. E. (2011), *What is a Do Not Resuscitate Order* (DNR), *http:// www.wisegeek.com/what-is-a-do-not-resuscitate-dnr-order.htm* (online access 29 May 2011) Stone, J. (2002), *An Ethical Framework for Complementary and Alternative Therapists*, London, Routledge. Stratton-Lake, P. (2002), '*Introduction*'. In Ross, W. D. 1930. The Right and the Good. Oxford: Oxford University Press. Sullivan, R. J. (1995), *An Introduction to Kant's Ethics*. Cambridge University Press. Sullivan, M. (2003), The new subjective medicine: taking the patient's point of view on health care and health. *Soc Sci Med* 56: 1595-604

Sweet, W. (2008), *Jeremy Bentham (1748-1832)*, Internet Encyclopedia of Philosophy, *www.iep.utm.edu/bentham*, (online access 14 April 2011)

Taboada, P. (2002), *Shaw's Criticism to the Double Effect Doctrine*, "http://www.hospicecare.com/Ethics/monthlypiece/eithics2002/ pom_oct.htm" (online access 20 January 2010)

Taboada, P. (2004), *Systematization of thee thicalanalysis of clinical cases*,   "http://www.hospicecare.com/Ethics/monthlypiece/ eithics2004/ pom_july04.htm" (online access 6 November 2009)

Taylor, B. (2010), *Professional Decision Making in social work practice*. Exeter, United Kingdom: Learning Matters.

Terry, J. (1977) 'Problems of teaching professional law to social workers', *The Law Teacher*, vol 11, no 1, pp 1-10.

Terry, L. (2007), *Ethics—Contemporary Challenges in Health and Social Care*. In: Leathhad, A. and McLaren, S. (Eds) Ethics—Contemporary Challenges in Health and Social Care. Bristol: Policy Press

Thompson, I., Melia K. M. and Boyd K. M. (2000), *Nursing ethics*, 4th edition. London: Churchill Livingstone.

Thompson, I., Melia, K., Boyd K. and Horsburgh, D. (2006) *Nursing Ethics*, 5th edition. Edinburgh: Churchill Livingstone.

Timpe, K. (2008), *Ethics* [Internet Encyclopedia of Philosophy], University of San Diego HYPERLINK "http://www.iep.utm.edu/ ethics" http://www.iep.utm.edu/ethics, (online access 4 December 2009)

Tingle, J. (2001), 'Patient power and litigiousness', *Practice Nursing*, vol 12, no 12, pp 487-8.

Tingle, J. and Cribb, A. (ed.) (2002), *Nursing Law and Ethics*, 2nd edition. Oxford: Blackwell Publishing.

Tong, R. (1997), *Feminist Approaches to Bioethics: Theoretical Reflections and Practical Applications.* Boulder, Colorado: Westview Press.

Tong, R. (2009), *Feminist Thought: A More Comprehensive Introduction.* Charlotte: Westview Press.

Tong, R. and William N. (2009), *Feminist Ethics*, Stanford Encyclopedia of philosophy, First published Tue May 12, 1998; substantive revision Monday, May 4, http://plato.stanford.edu/entries/feminism-ethics/#2, (online access 28 July 2010)

Tremayne, P. (2008), *Learning Nursing*. In: Hincliff, S., Norman, S. and Schober, J. (eds.) Nursing Practice and Healthcare, A Foundation Text, 5th edition. London: Edward Arnold Ltd.

Tsai, D. F. (1999), *Ancient Chinese Medical Ethics and four principles of biomedical ethics*, J. Med. Ethics, *http://jme.bmj.com/cgi/reprint/25/4/315.pdf* (online access 28 October 2009)

Tschudin, V. Ed. (1994), *Conflicts of interest*. Middlesex: Scutari Press (p. vii)

Tschudin, V (1999), *Nurses Matter, Reclaiming our Professional Identity*, London, Macmillan Press Ltd.

Tschudin, V. (2003), *Ethics in nursing: The caring relationship.* London: Elsevier science.

Tweeddale, M. G. (2002), Grasping the nettle—what to do when patients withdraw their consent for treatment: (a clinical perspective on the case of Ms B). *Journal Medical Ethics* 28(4): 236-7

Twomey, R. (2009), *Mind: Abuse by health and social care workers*, http://www.mind.org.uk/help/community_care/abuse (online access 10 November 2009)

UNICEF (2008), *Conventions on the rights of the child*, www.unicef.org (online access 17 July 2009).

United Nations Office of the High Commissioner for Human Rights (1989), *Convention on the Rights of the Child*, www2.ohchr.org/english/law/crc, (Online access, 10 July 2009).

Velasquez, M., Andre, C., Thomas-Shanks, S. J., and Meyer, M. J. (2010), *Thinking Ethically: A Framework for Moral Decision Making*, *http://www.scu.edu/ethics/practicing/decision/thinking.html* (online access 30 April 2010)

Waine, B.,Tunstill, J., Meadows, P., and Peel, M. (2005), *Developing Social Care: Values and Principles, Social Care Institute for Excellence*, Policy Press, Bristol

Wallenmaier, T. (2007), *Philosophy Class, www.philopshyclass.com/ethics* (online access 6 November 2009)

Walters, H. (2008), *Gillick competency or Fraser guidelines*, http://www.nspcc.org.uk (online access 9 July 2009).

Weller, B. F. (2005), *Balliere's Nurses Dictionary*, 24th edition, London, Elsevier (p. 92)

Wells, J. K. (2007), *Ethical Dilemma and Resolution*: a case scenario, January-March 4 (1) Indian Journal of Medical Ethics, *www.issuesinmedicalethics.org/151cs31.html*, (online access 28 July 2010)

Wilson, F. (2007), "John Stuart Mill," The Stanford Encyclopedia of Philosophy (First published Thu Jan 3, 2002; substantive revision Tue Jul 10, 2007 *http://plato.stanford.edu/archives/spr2009/entries/mill*, (online access 28 July 2010)

Woolrich, C. (2008), *Principles of Professional Practice*. In: Hincliff, S., Norman, S., and Schober, J. (eds.) Nursing Practice and Healthcare, A Foundation Text, 5th edition. London: Edward Arnold Ltd, www.ncbi.nlm.nih.gov/pubmed?term=per   cent22Zomorodi   (online access 10 February 2010)

INDEX